CROWNS

TREASURE TROVE OF LAVISH DESIGNS

BY PAMELA L. CLAUSSEN

Publisher: Pamela L. Claussen
Designer: Pamela L. Claussen
Editor: Pamela L. Claussen
Photographer: Alex Hayden
Graphic artist: Stephanie Belcher

Printed in the United States by Walsworth Publishing

www.GlamByPam.net
pc@glambypam.net

ISBN-10: 0-9793297-0-1
ISBN-13: 978-0-9793297-0-8

Dedication

To my father, Delmar LaVerne Gibbons,
I miss you and think of you every day.

To my husband, John, the love of my life,
and my son Tony of whom I'm so proud.

Acknowledgements

To the late Stella Reeves for 14 years of friendship
and the vintage rhinestones that kept this passion alive.

To Margaret Powell Phillips for her magical ribbonwork.

And to the craftspeople who have throughout
history woven, dyed or styled textiles,
and have found in a single thread or stitch,
extreme beauty.

Forward

I think I was meant to be a Victorian woman.

From the age of 12, a quiet side of me was drawn to rich fabrics, a sprig of ribbon, gleaming rhinestones and gems. Looking into my Grandmother Velma's jewelry drawer was a wonderland. I have some of her necklaces and brooches, still. I could pretend I was a princess, and dress up in lace and hats from mother's closet. She bought a hope chest, and I imagined it full of my own finery.

It wasn't until decades later that this rhapsody over frills became a passion for making headpieces. Inspired by Victorian wedding skull caps that flaunt their ultra femininity, I envisioned how exquisite beaded hats could cross the centuries into something new, but equally timeless.

So I went to my hope chest. By now it was filled with antique ribbons culled from street markets in Paris, my Aunt Lucy's pearls, antique and vintage amethysts and rhinestones, scraps of era wedding dresses and silk pantaloons. Simply for my own expression and enjoyment, I created each headpiece layer by layer. Each piece became a unique radiant sculpture.

It is my pleasure to share this inspiration with you. Hopefully it will move you to collect remnants from armoires of the women in your past and piece together your own heirloom.

Be dazzled. I continue to be.

Table of Contents

Tiaras
Plate 1 to 54

Headbands with Veil Attachment
Plate 307 to 334

Skull Caps
Plate 55 to 98

Full Circle Headbands
Plate 335 to 398

Pillbox Hats
Plate 99 to 266

Hats
Plate 399 to 404

Headbands
Plate 267 to 306

Antique Tiaras
Plate 405 to 412

French Wedding Globes

Tiaras

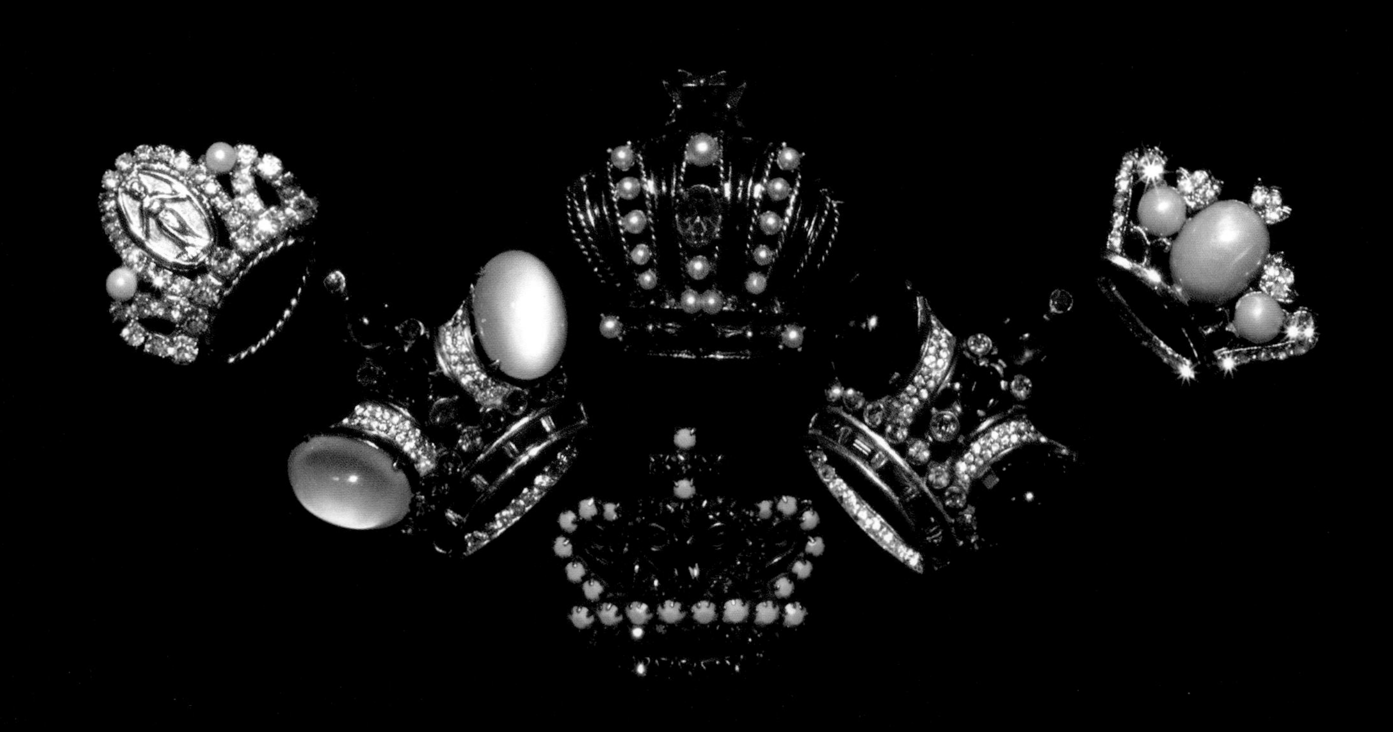

Plate 001

Plate 004

Plate 005

PLATE 006

Plate 007

PLATE 008

Plate 009

PLATE 010

PLATE 011

PLATE 012

Plate 013

PLATE 014

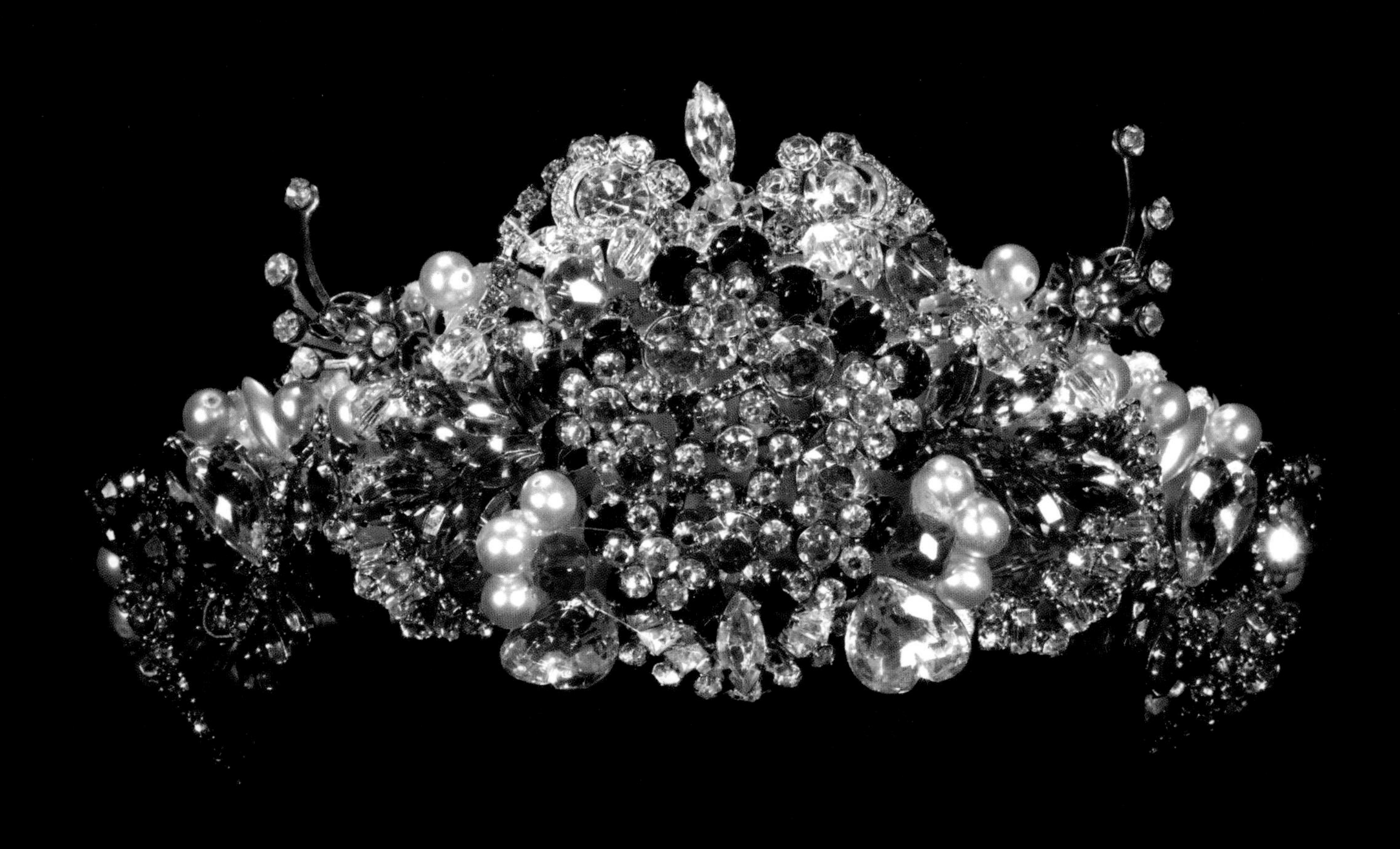

PLATE 015

PLATE 016

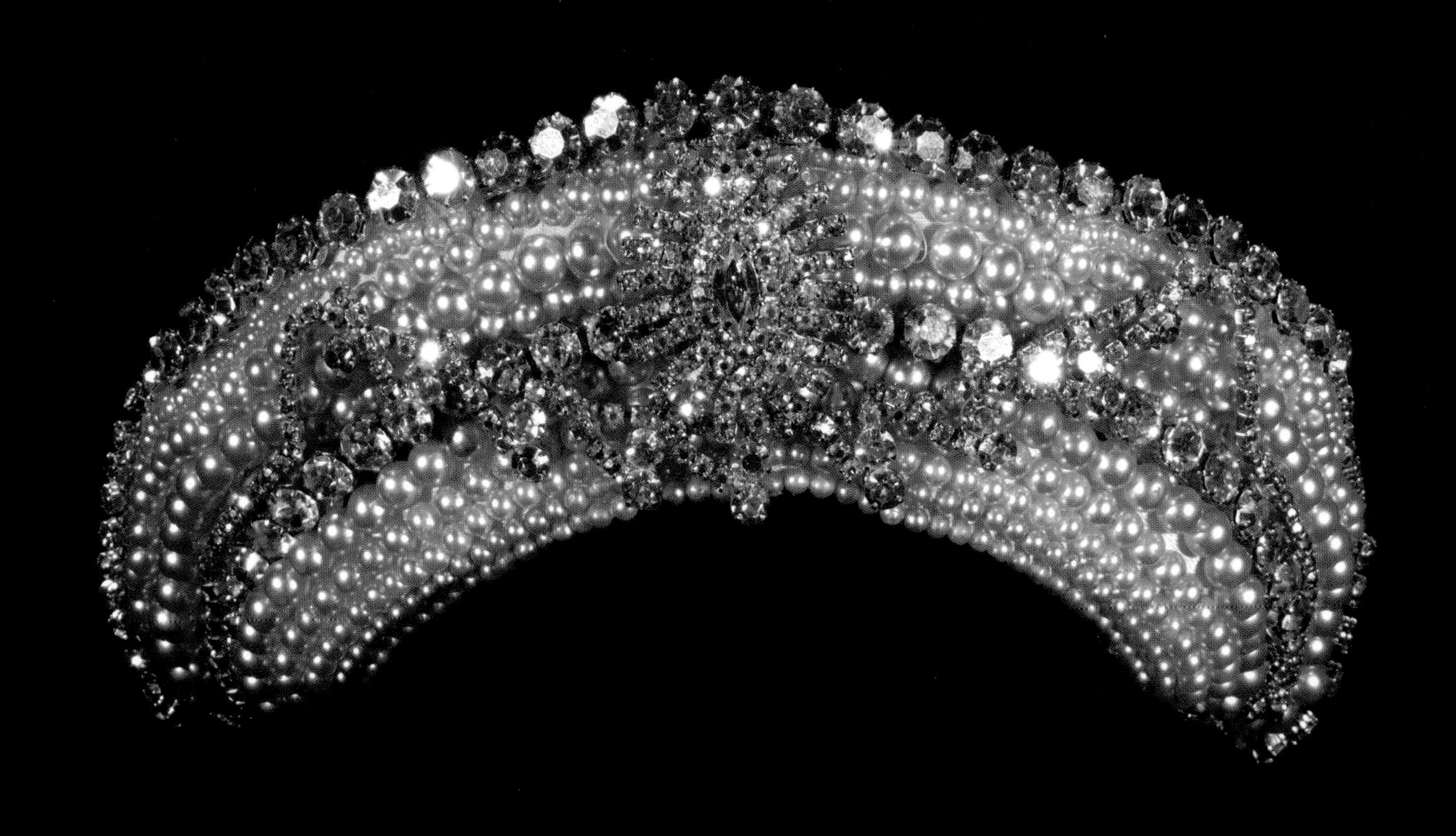

PLATE 017

Plate 018

PLATE 019

Plate 020

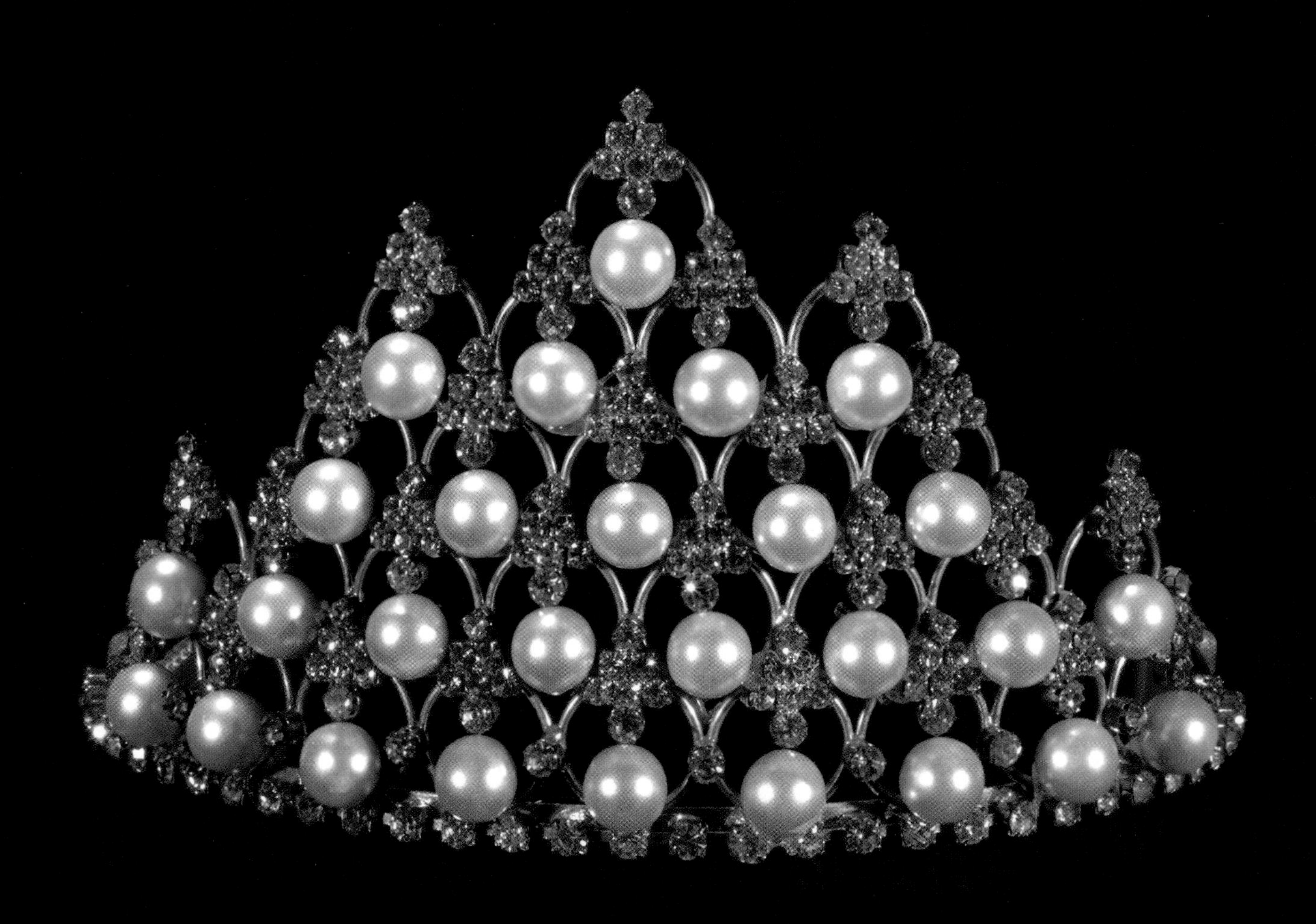

Plate 021

Plate 022

Plate 023

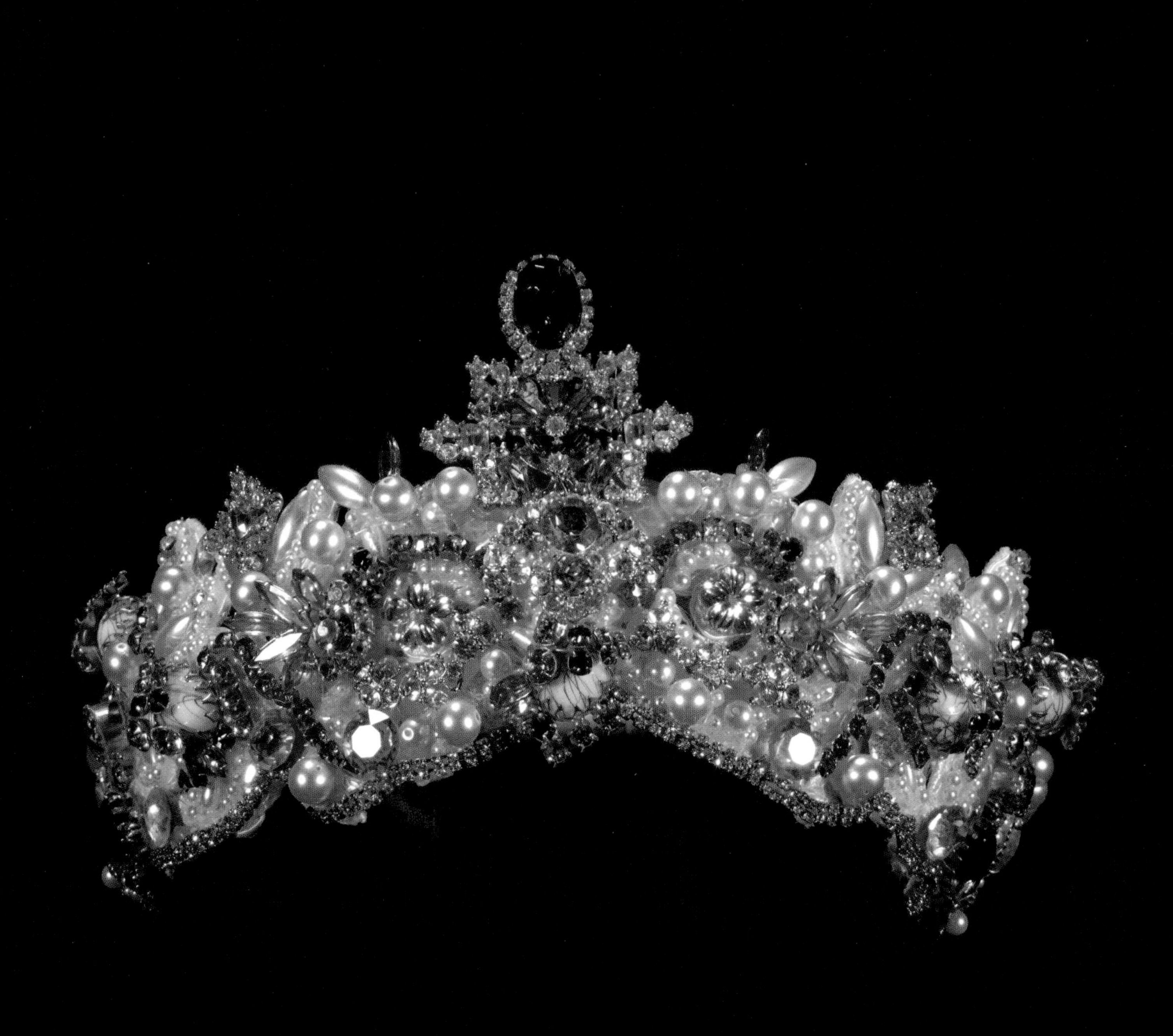

Plate 024

Plate 025

PLATE 026

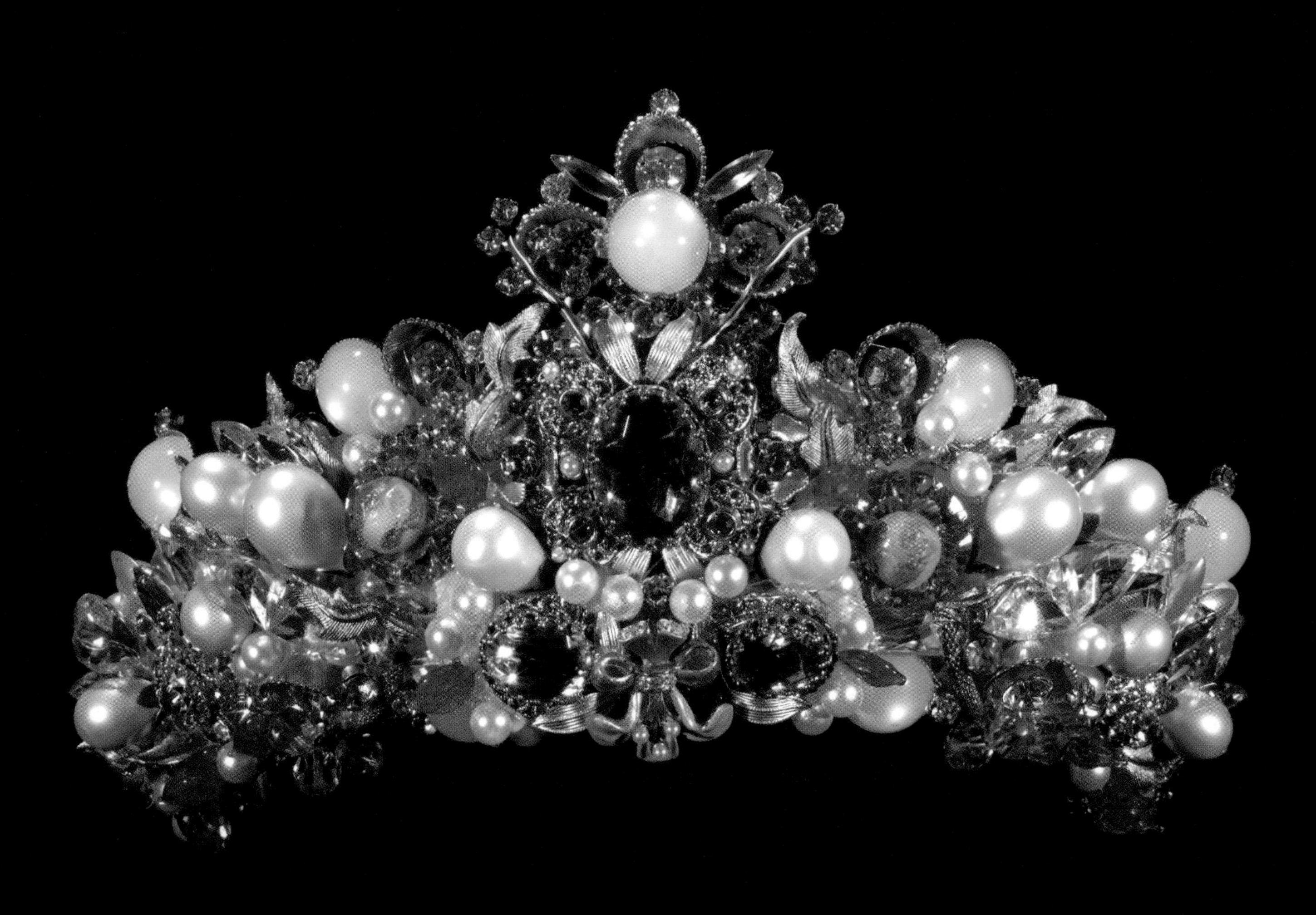

Plate 027

Plate 028

Plate 029

Plate 030

PLATE 031

PLATE 032

Plate 033

Plate 034

PLATE 035

Plate 036

Plate 037

Plate 038

PLATE 039

Plate 040

PLATE 041

Plate 042

Plate 043

PLATE 044

PLATE 045

Plate 046

PLATE 047

Plate 048

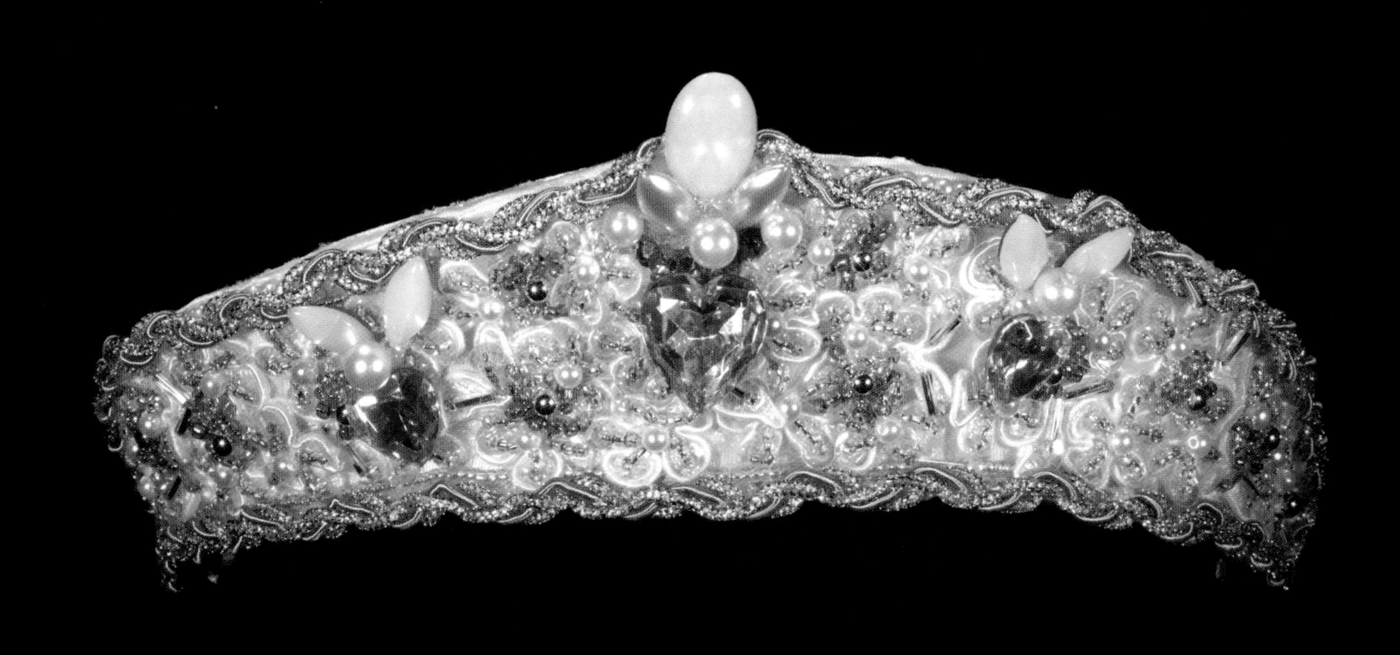

PLATE 049

PLATE 050

PLATE 051

Plate 052

Plate 053

PLATE 054

Skullcaps

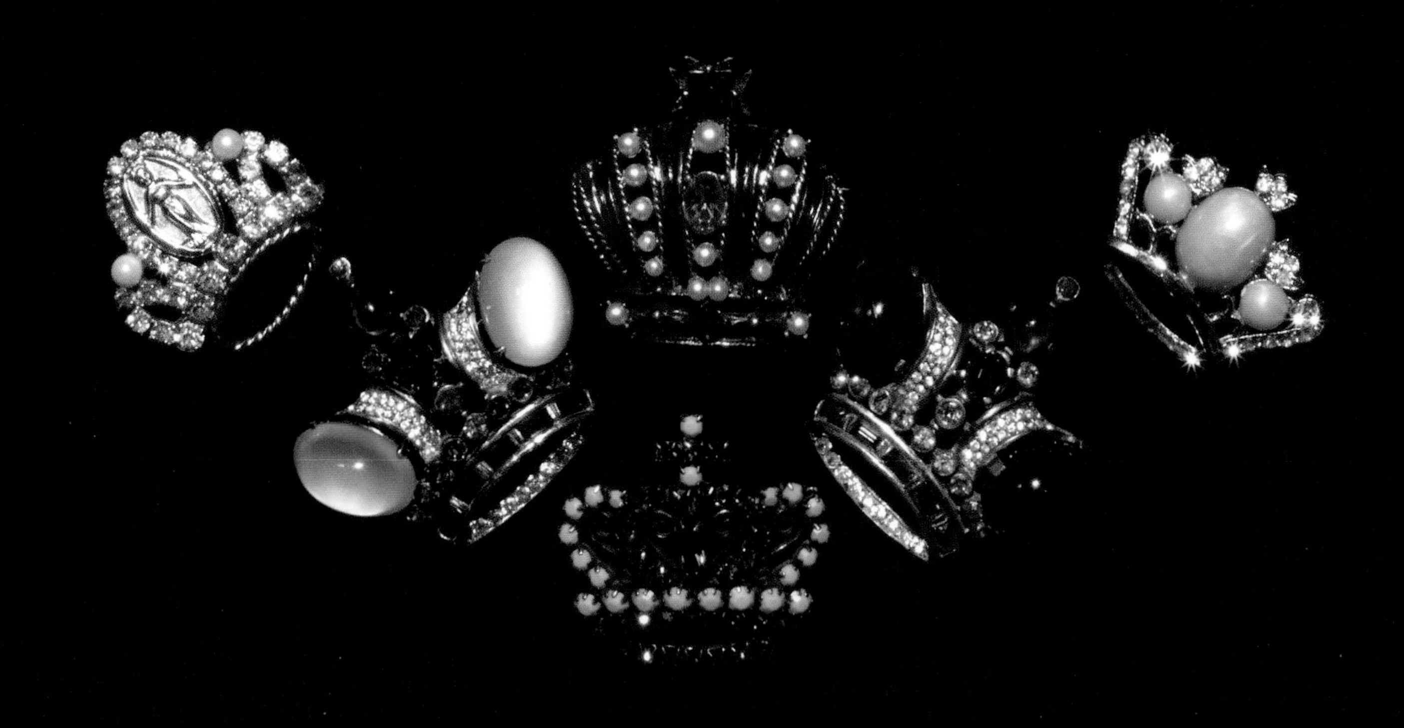

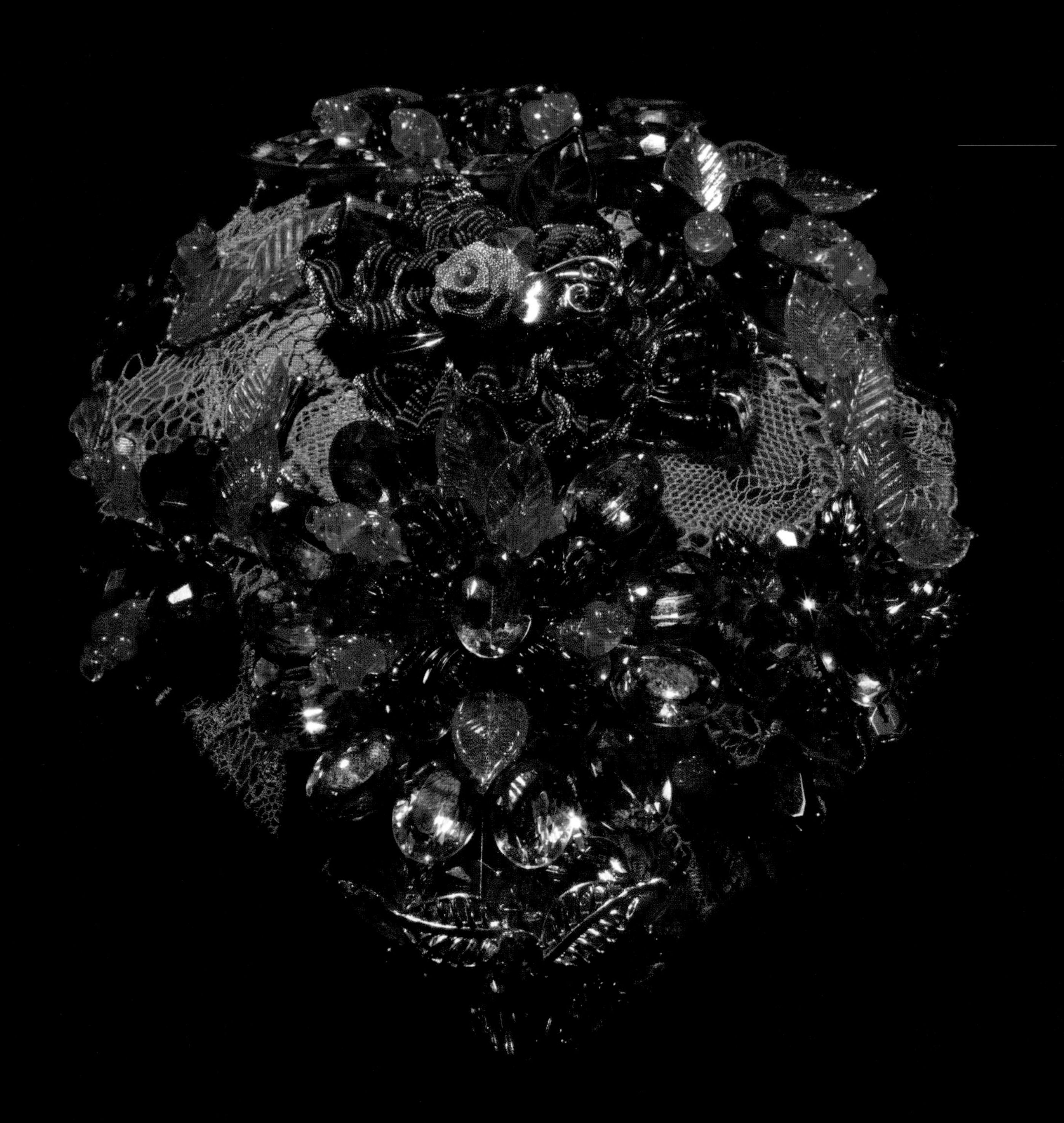

Plate 055

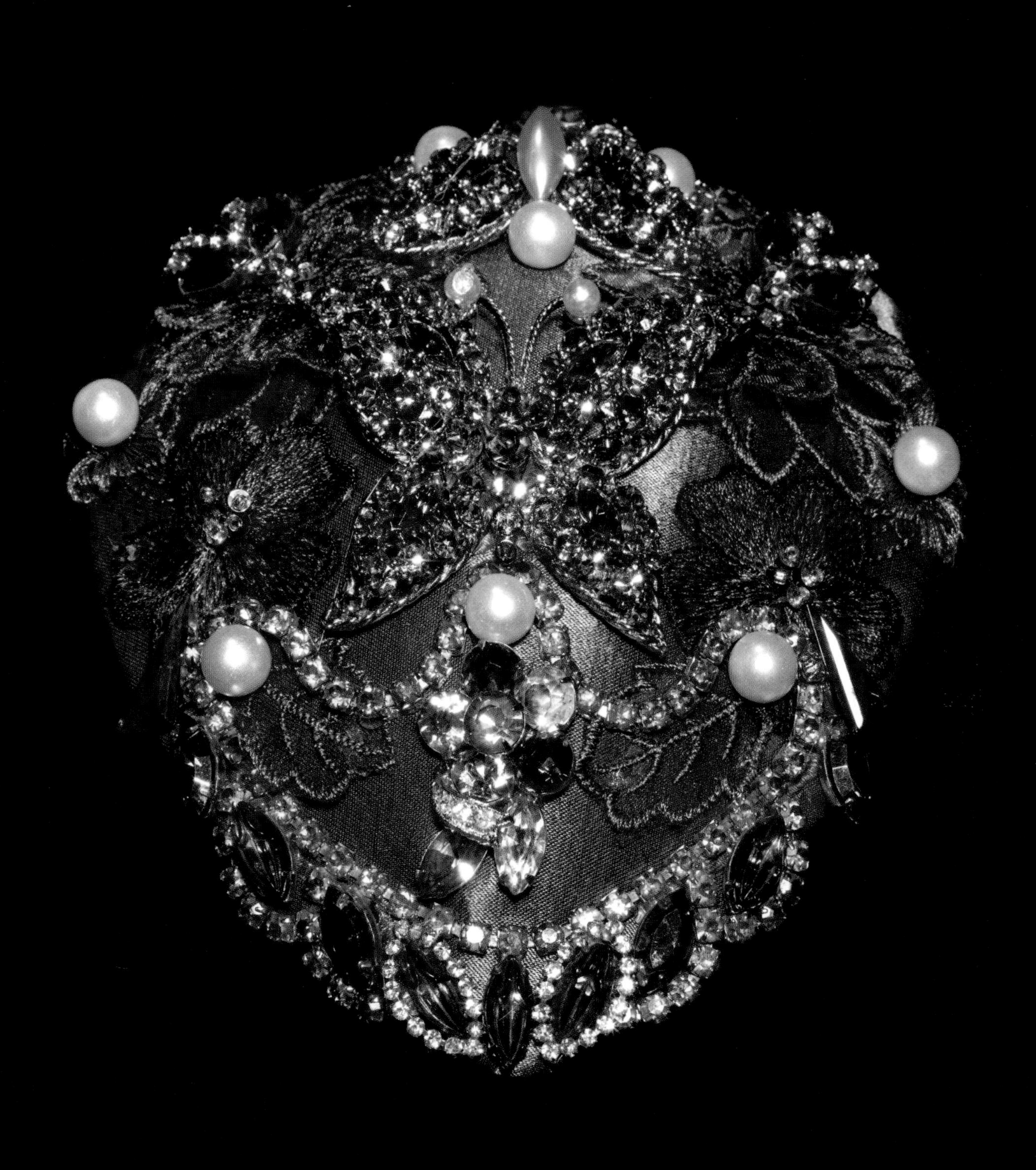

PLATE 056

PLATE 057

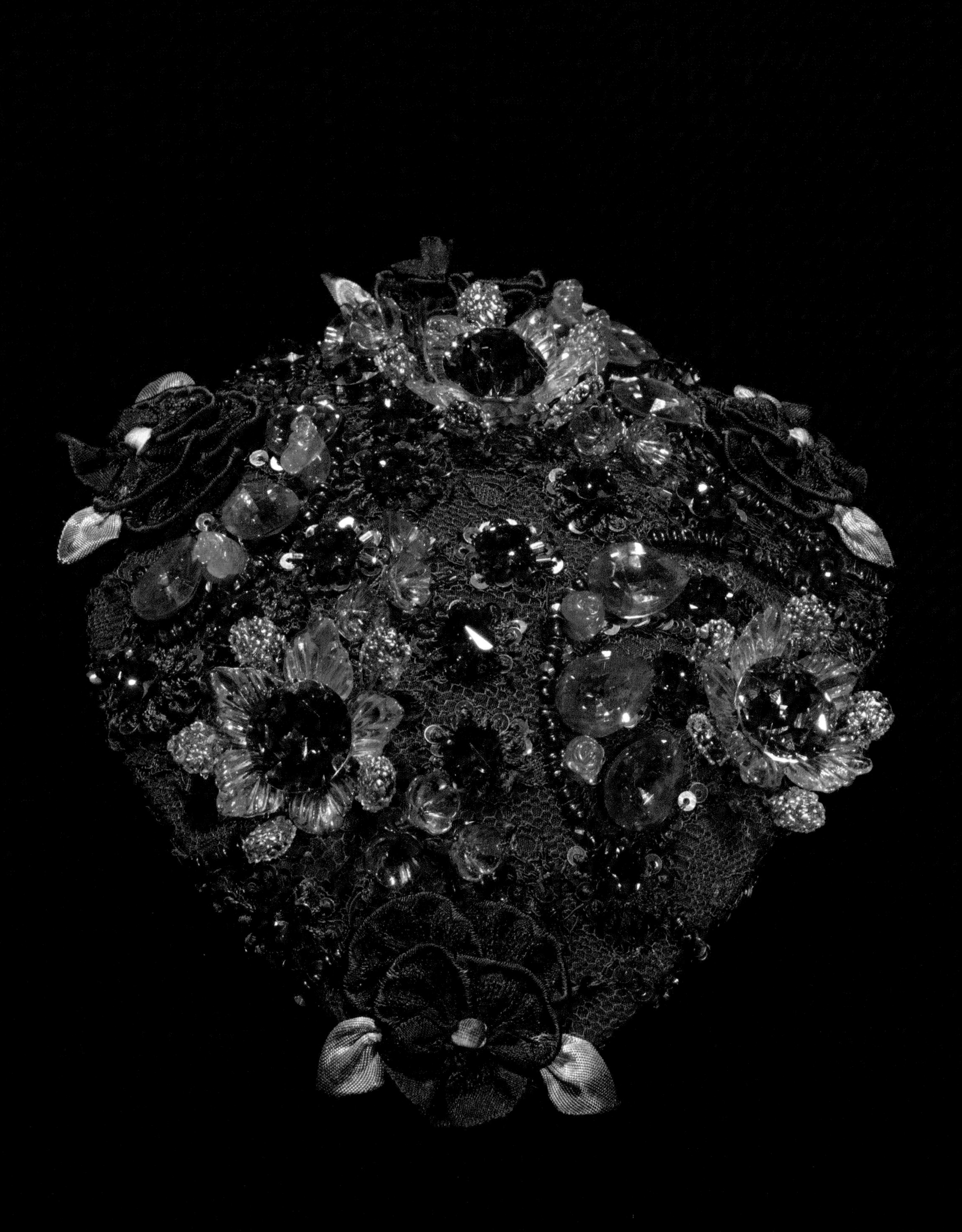

Plate 058

Plate 059

Plate 060

PLATE 061

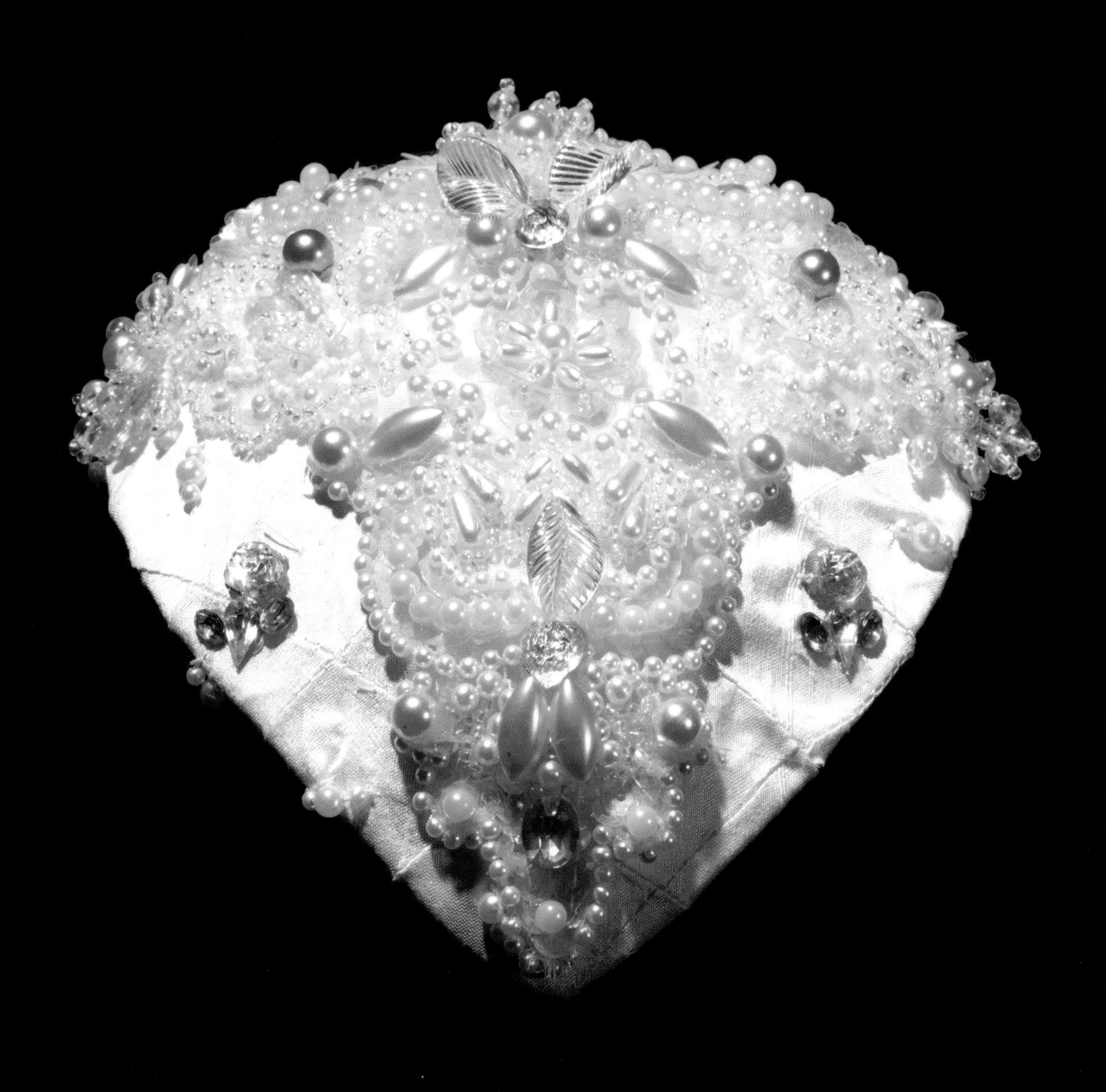

Plate 062

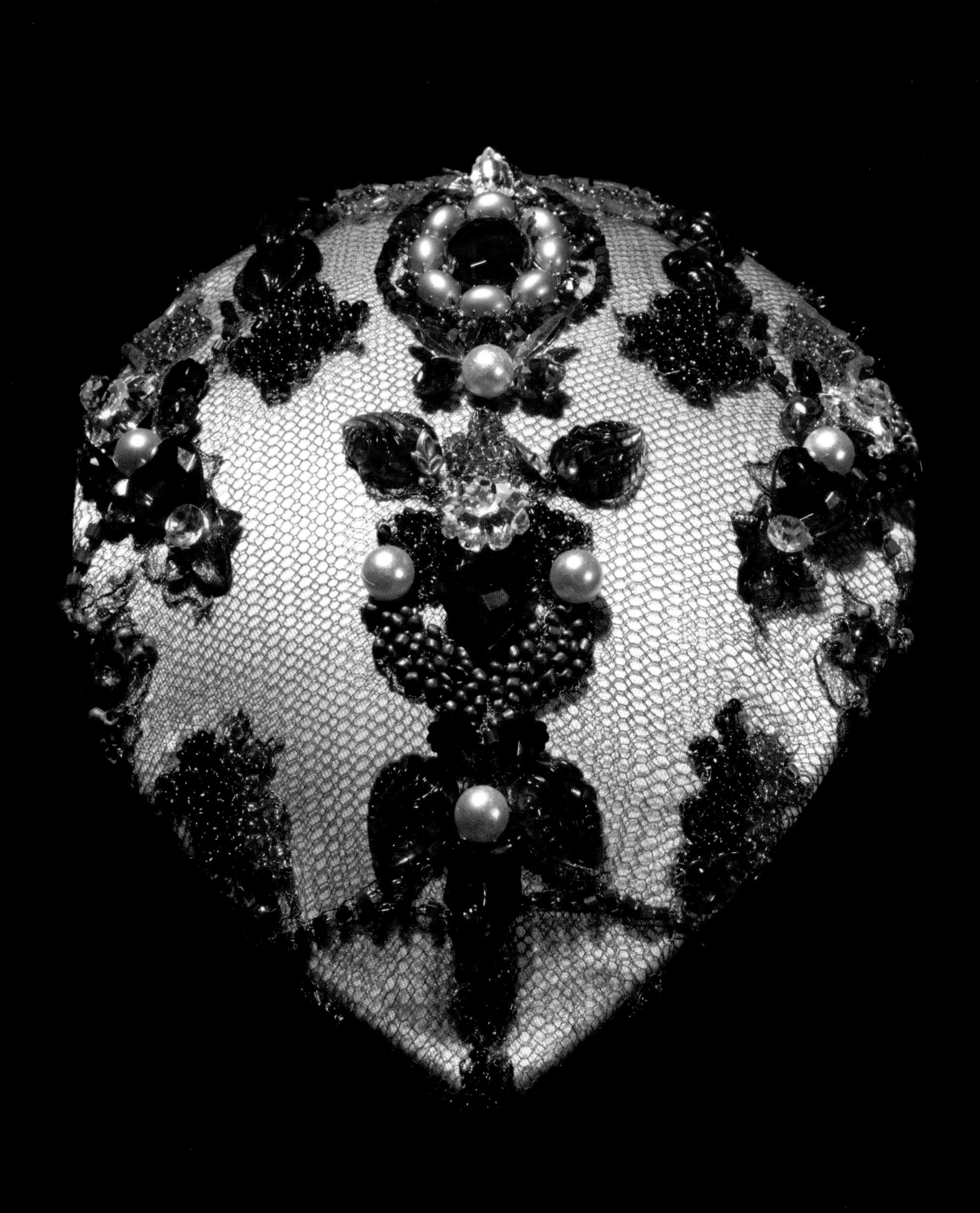

Plate 063

PLATE 064

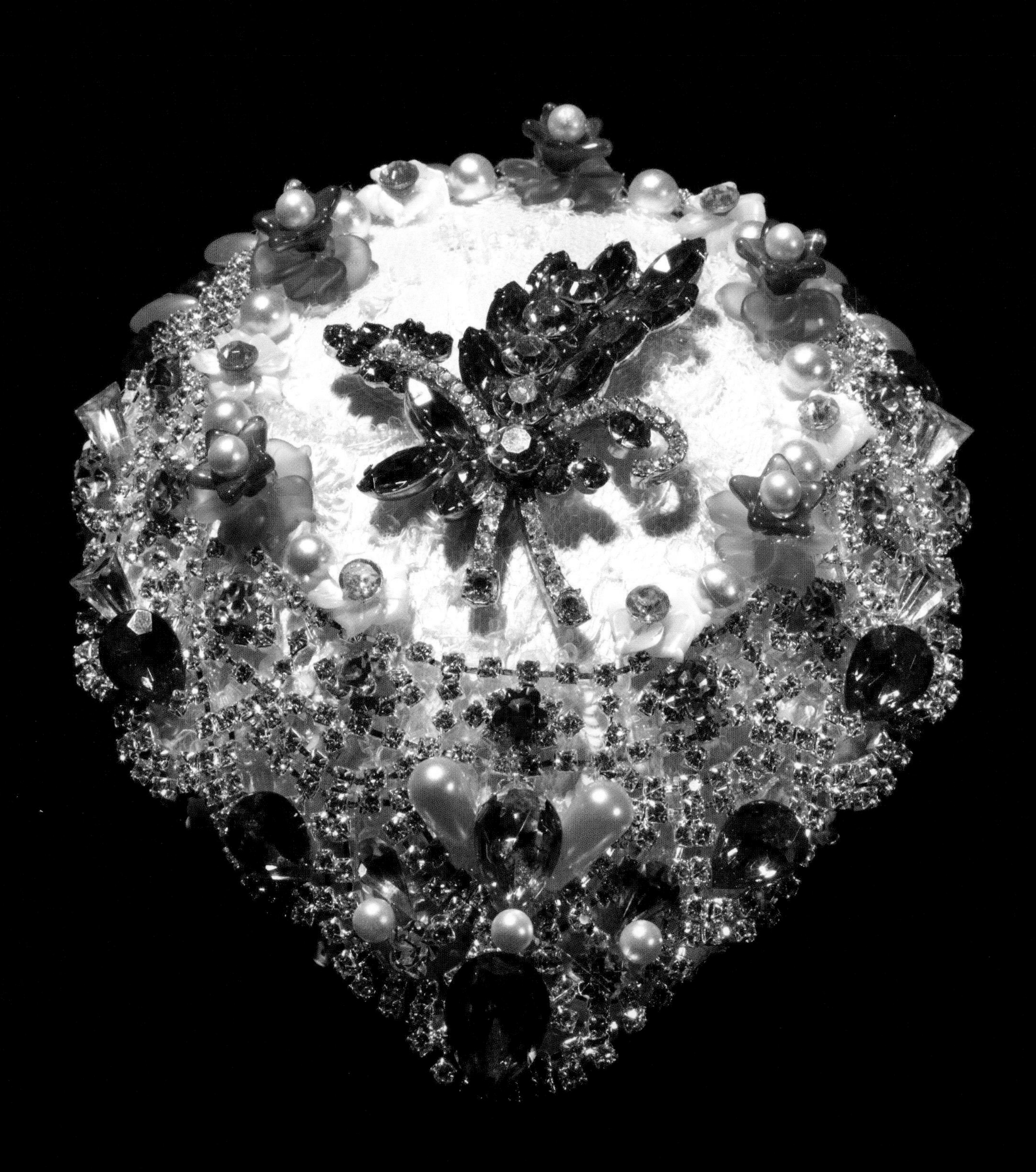

PLATE 065

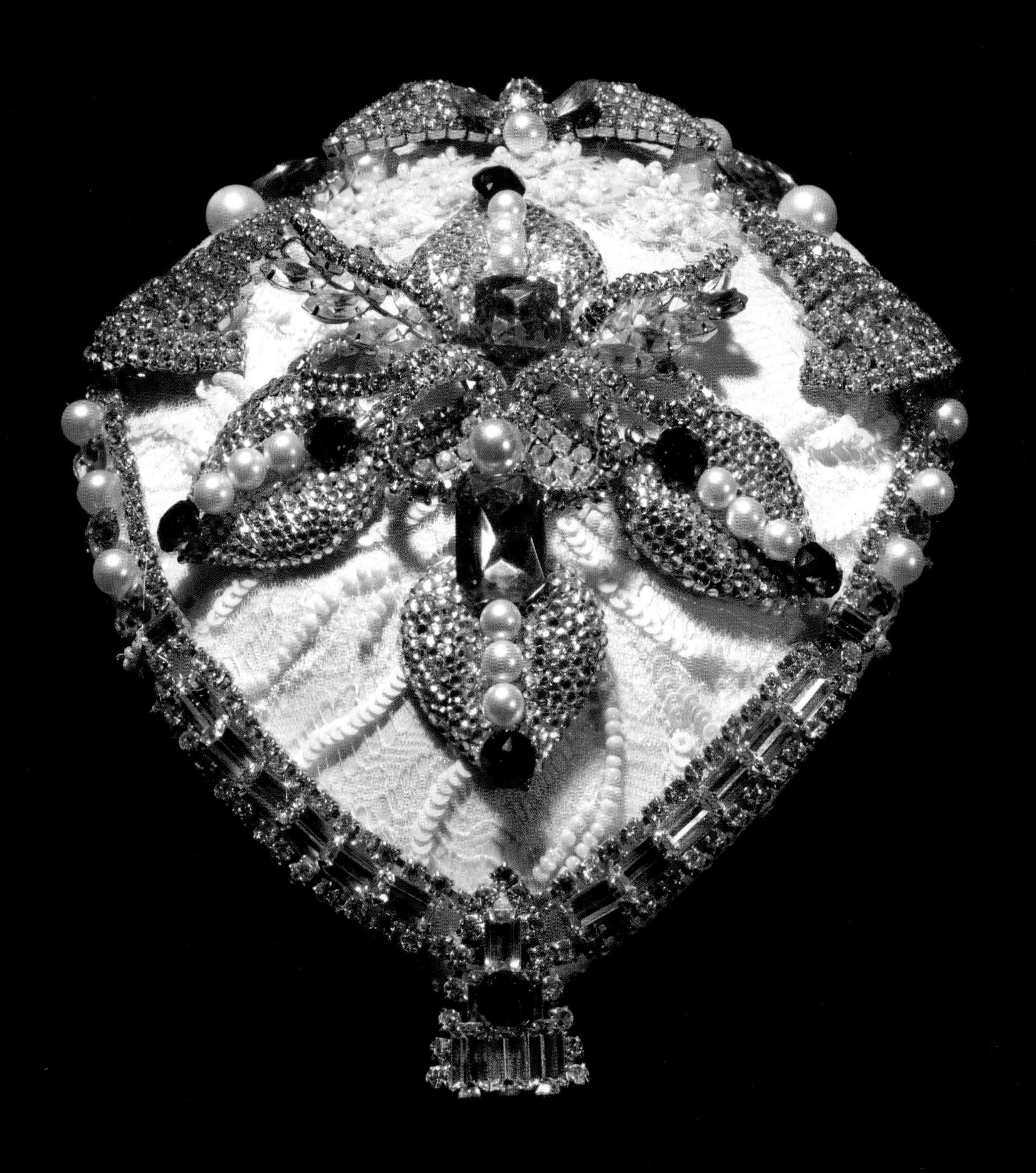

Plate 066

Plate 067

PLATE 068

PLATE 069

Plate 070

PLATE 071

Plate 072

PLATE 073

Plate 074

Plate 075

PLATE 076

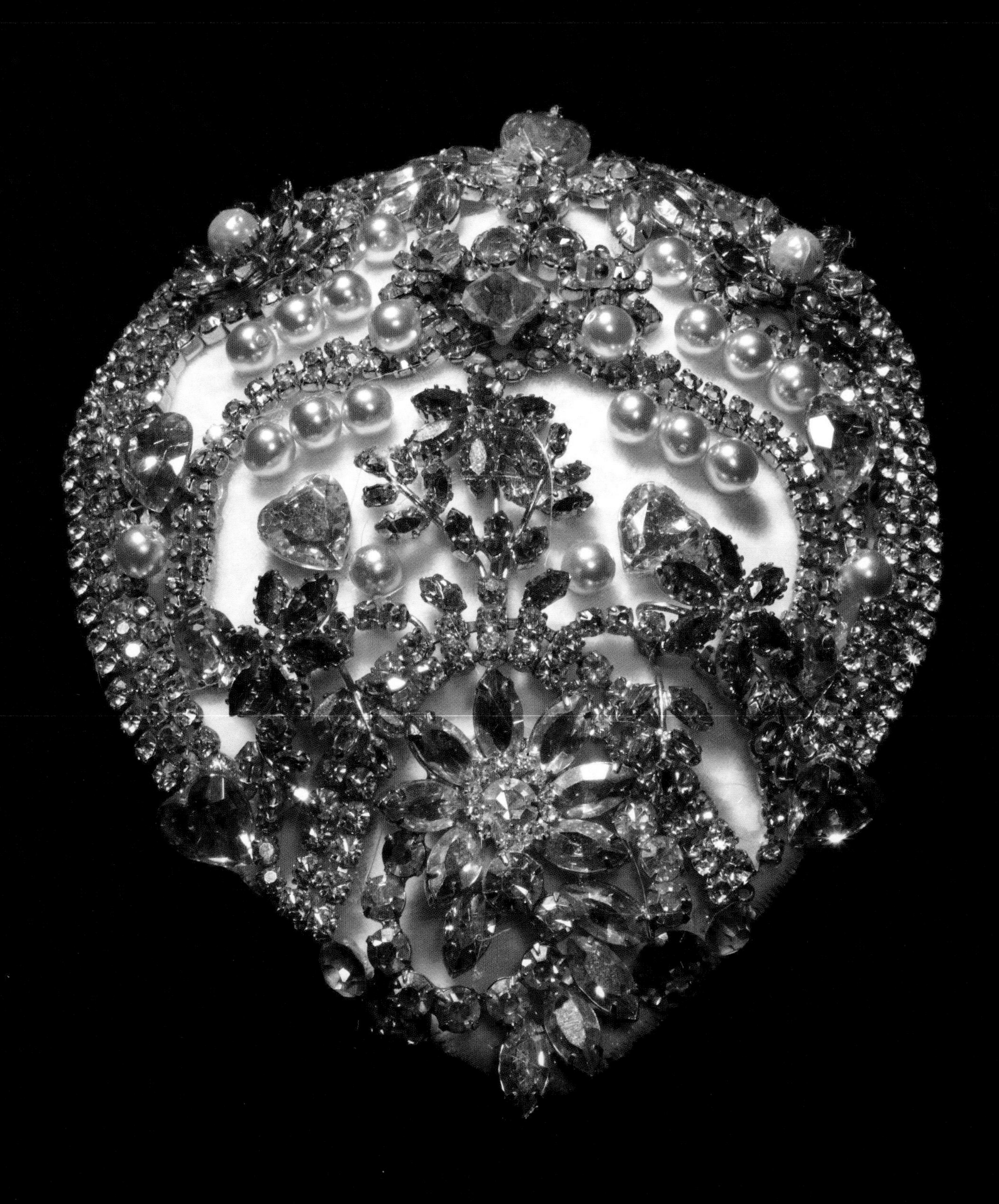

Plate 077

PLATE 078

Plate 079

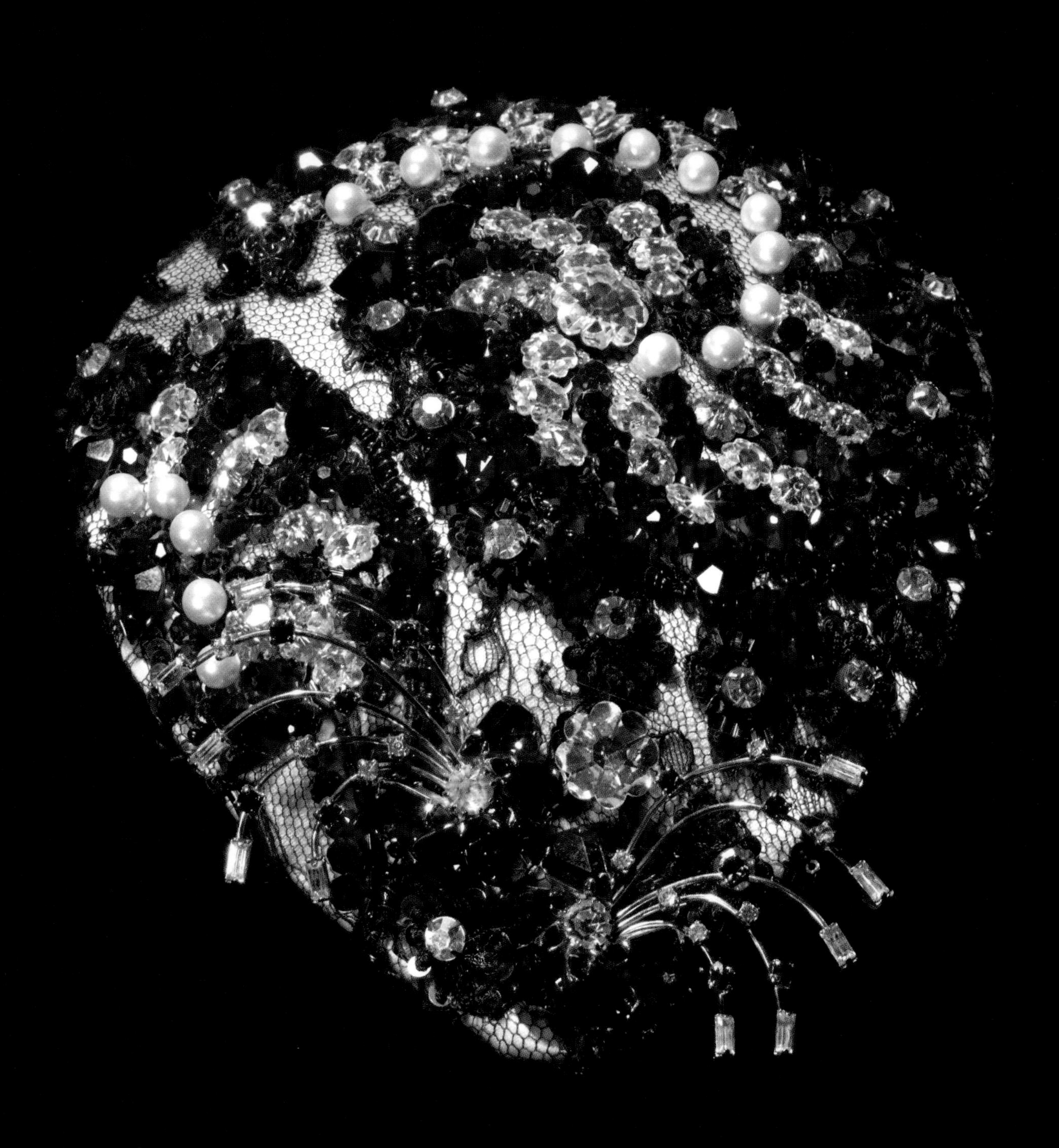

Plate 080

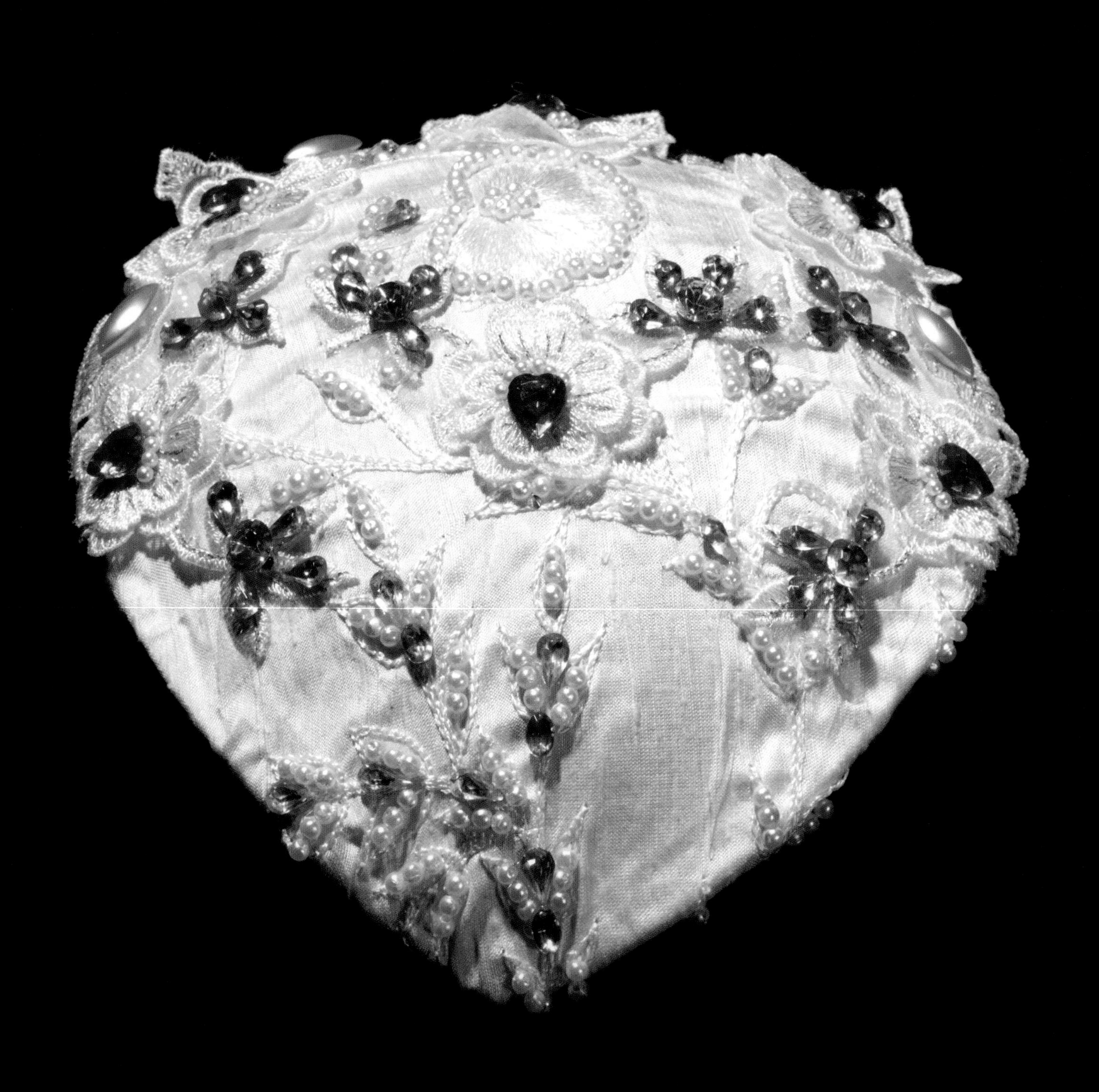

PLATE 081

Plate 082

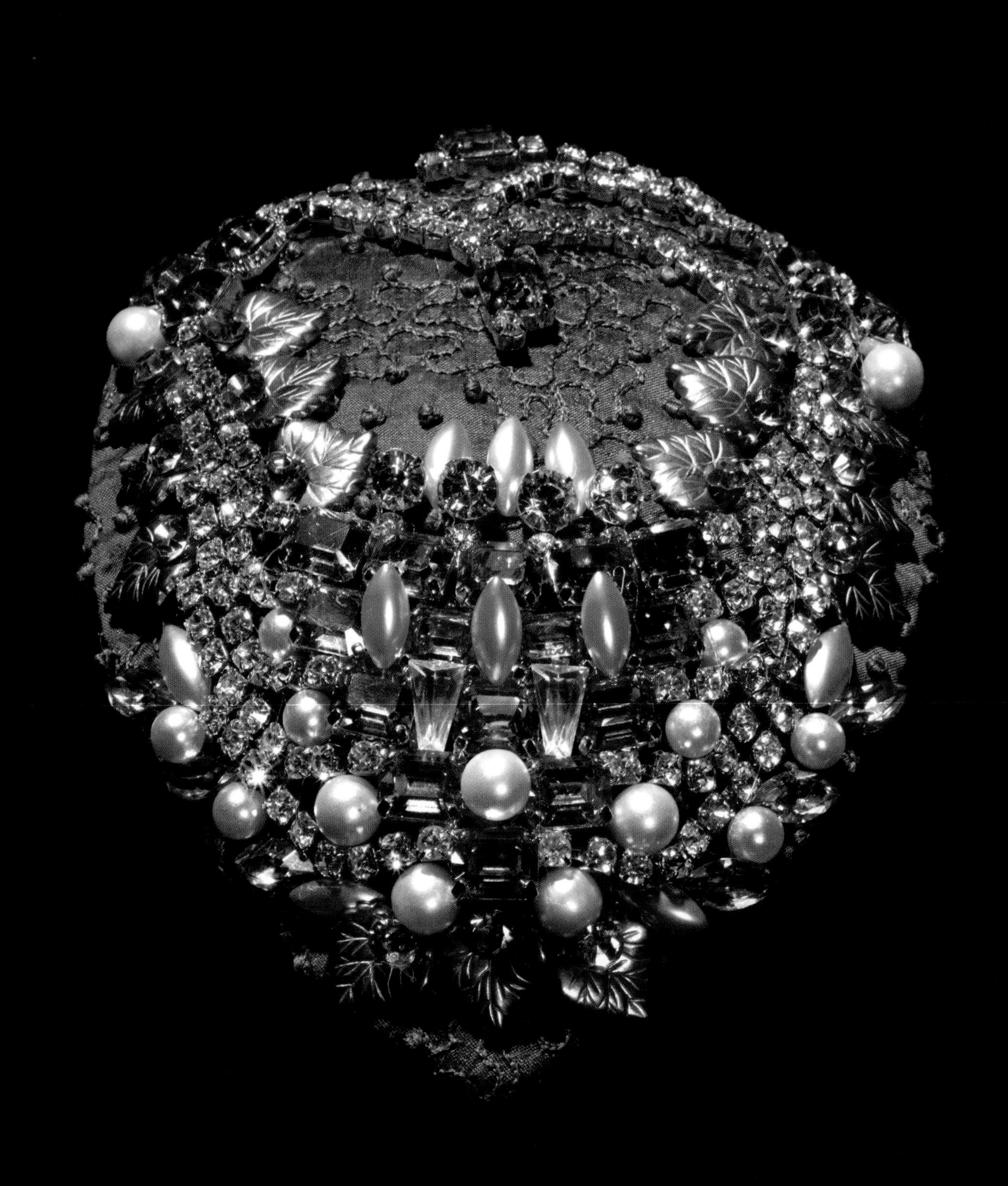

PLATE 083

PLATE 084

Plate 085

Plate 086

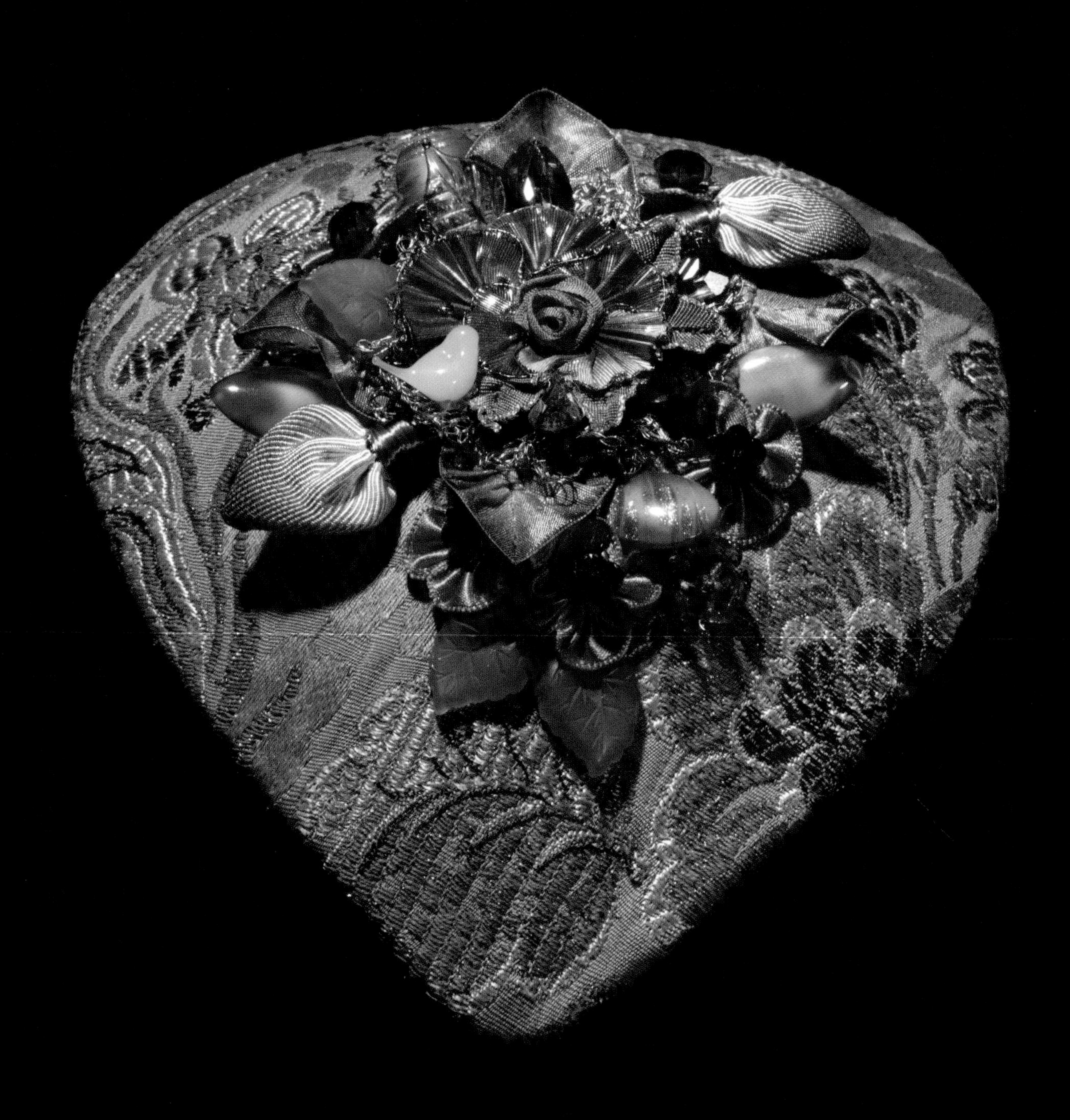

PLATE 087

PLATE 088

PLATE 089

Plate 090

PLATE 091

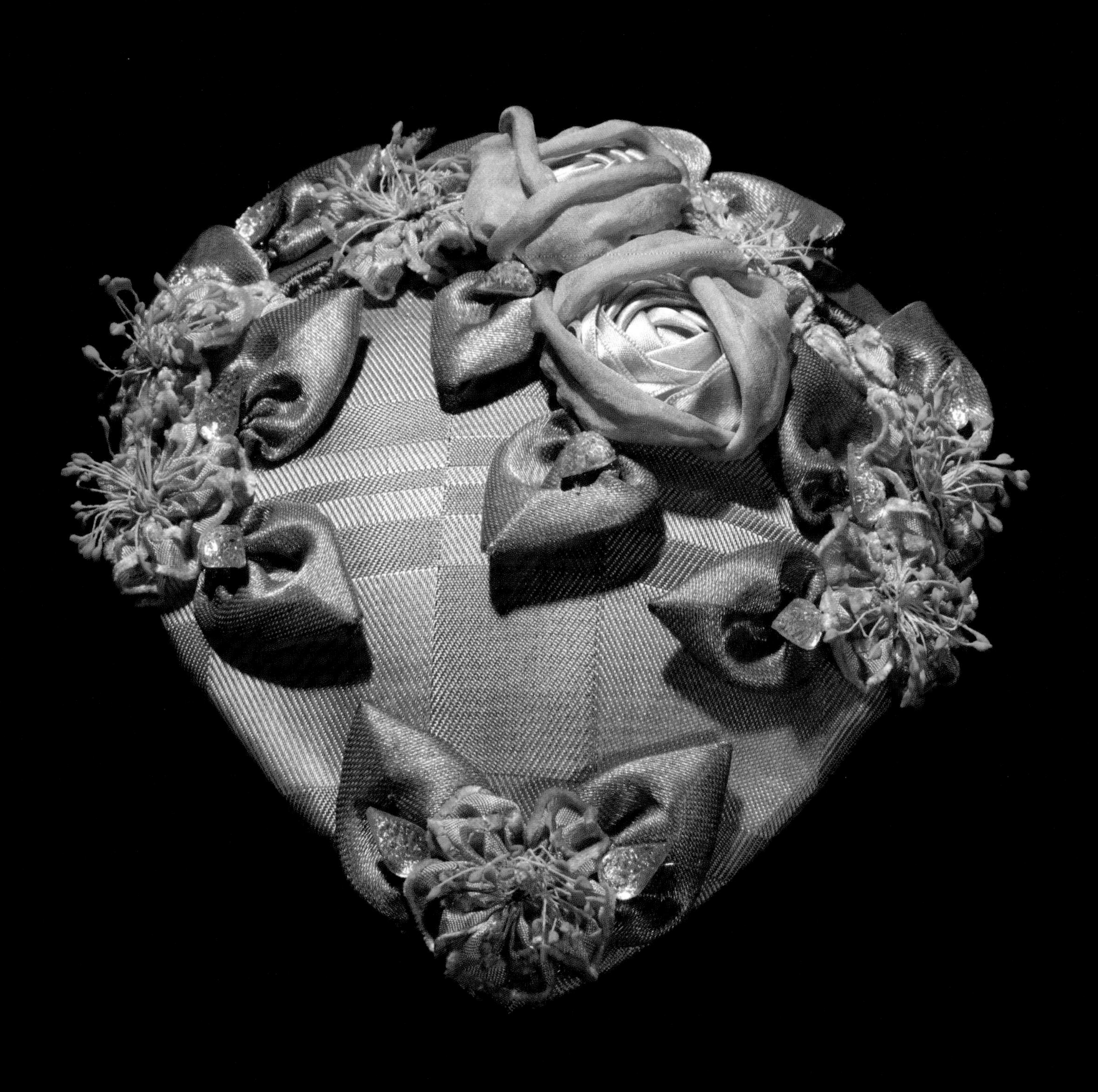

Plate 092

PLATE 093

PLATE 094

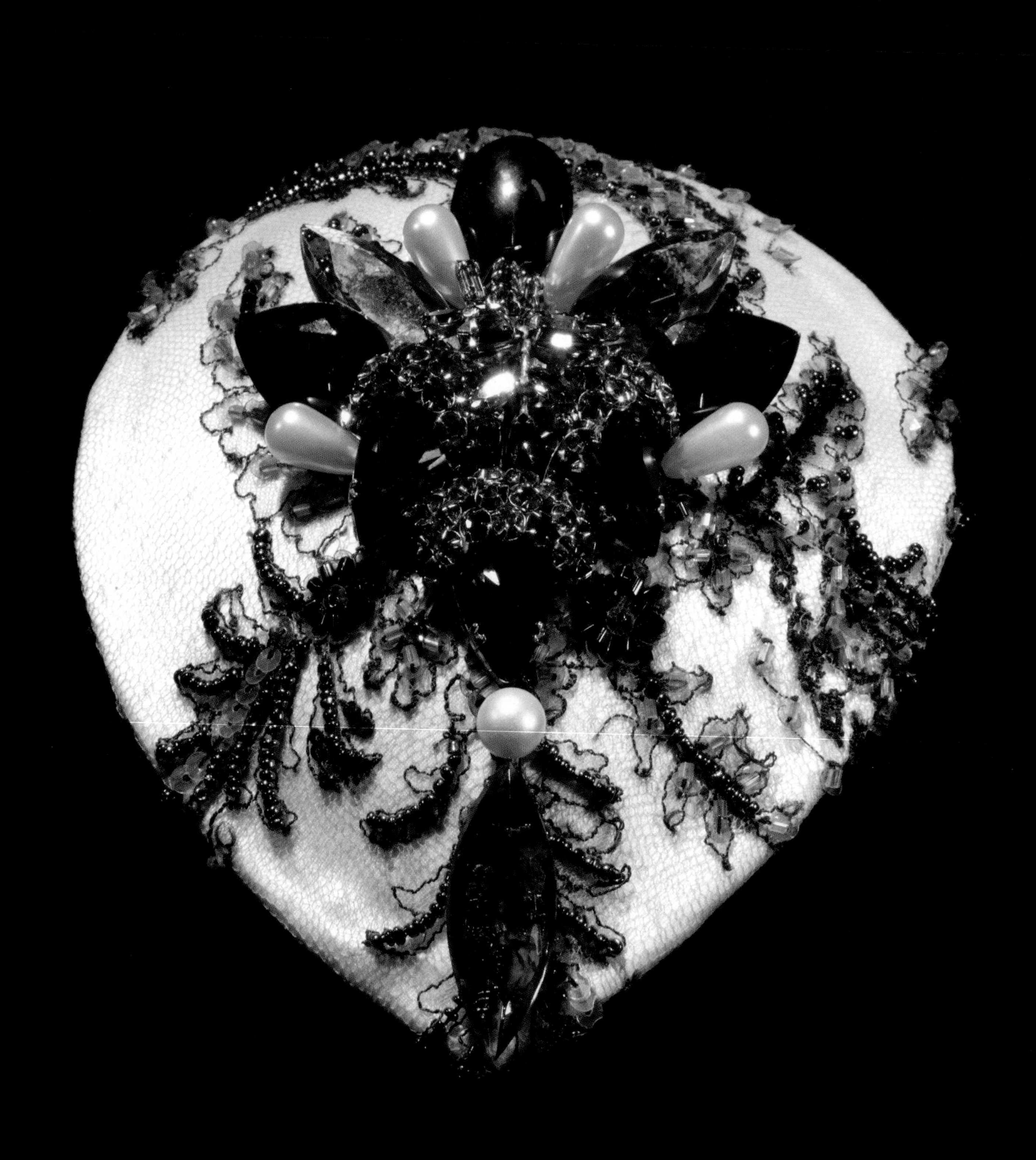

PLATE 095

PLATE 096

Plate 097

PLATE 098

Pillbox Hats

PLATE 099

Plate 100

PLATE 101

PLATE 102

PLATE 103

PLATE 104

Plate 105

Plate 106

Plate 107

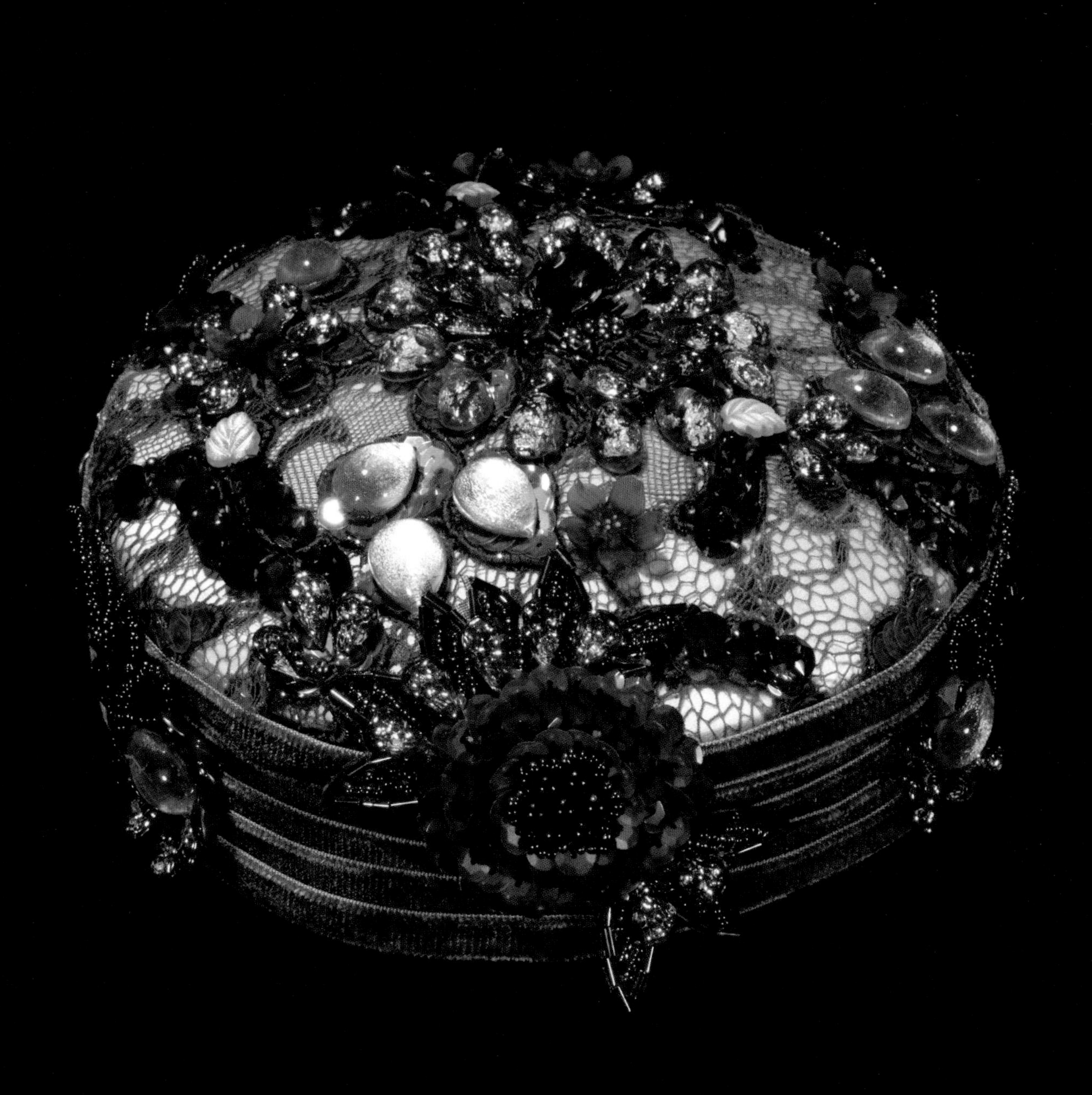

Plate 108

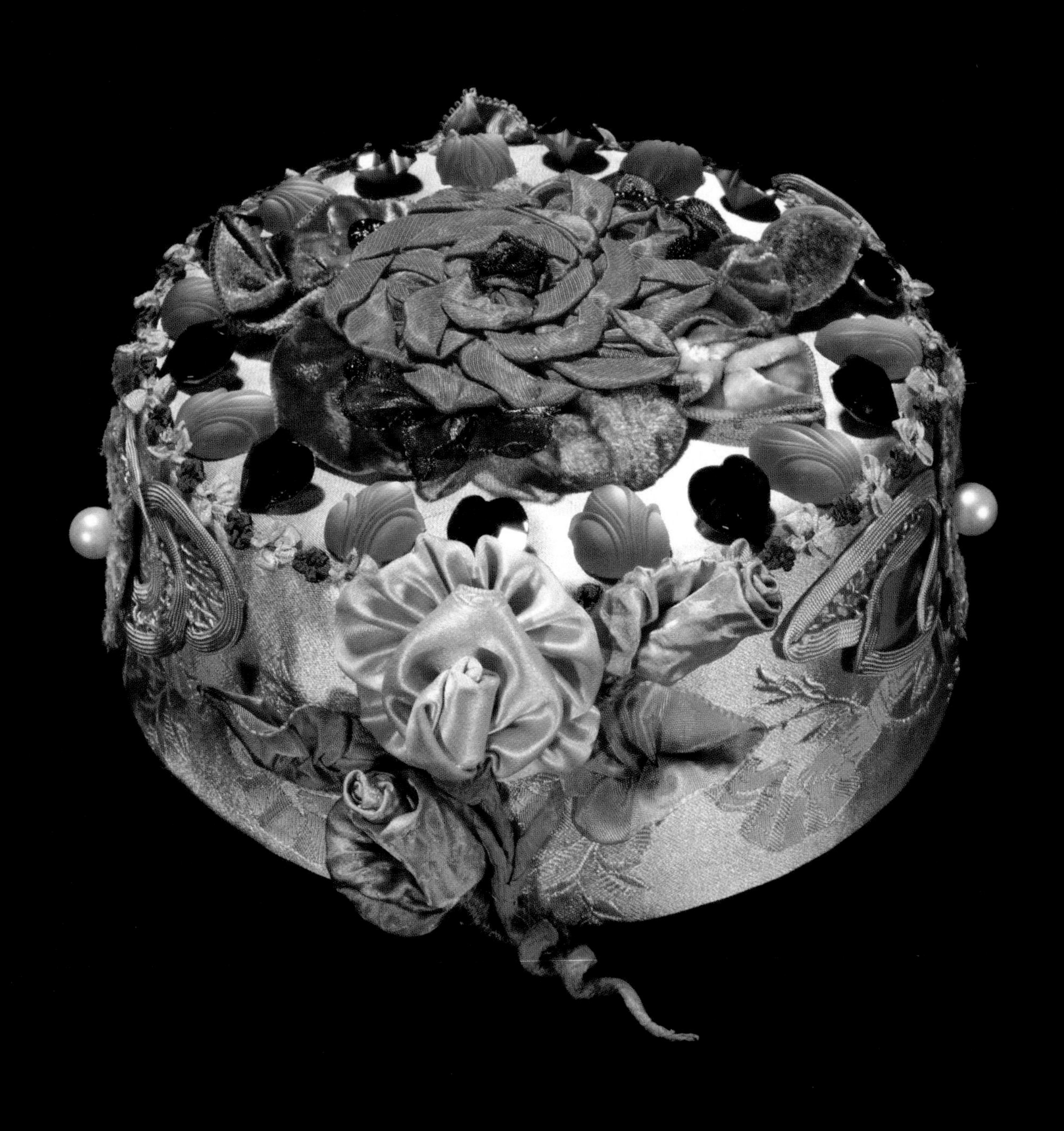

PLATE 109

Plate 110

Plate 111

Plate 112

PLATE 113

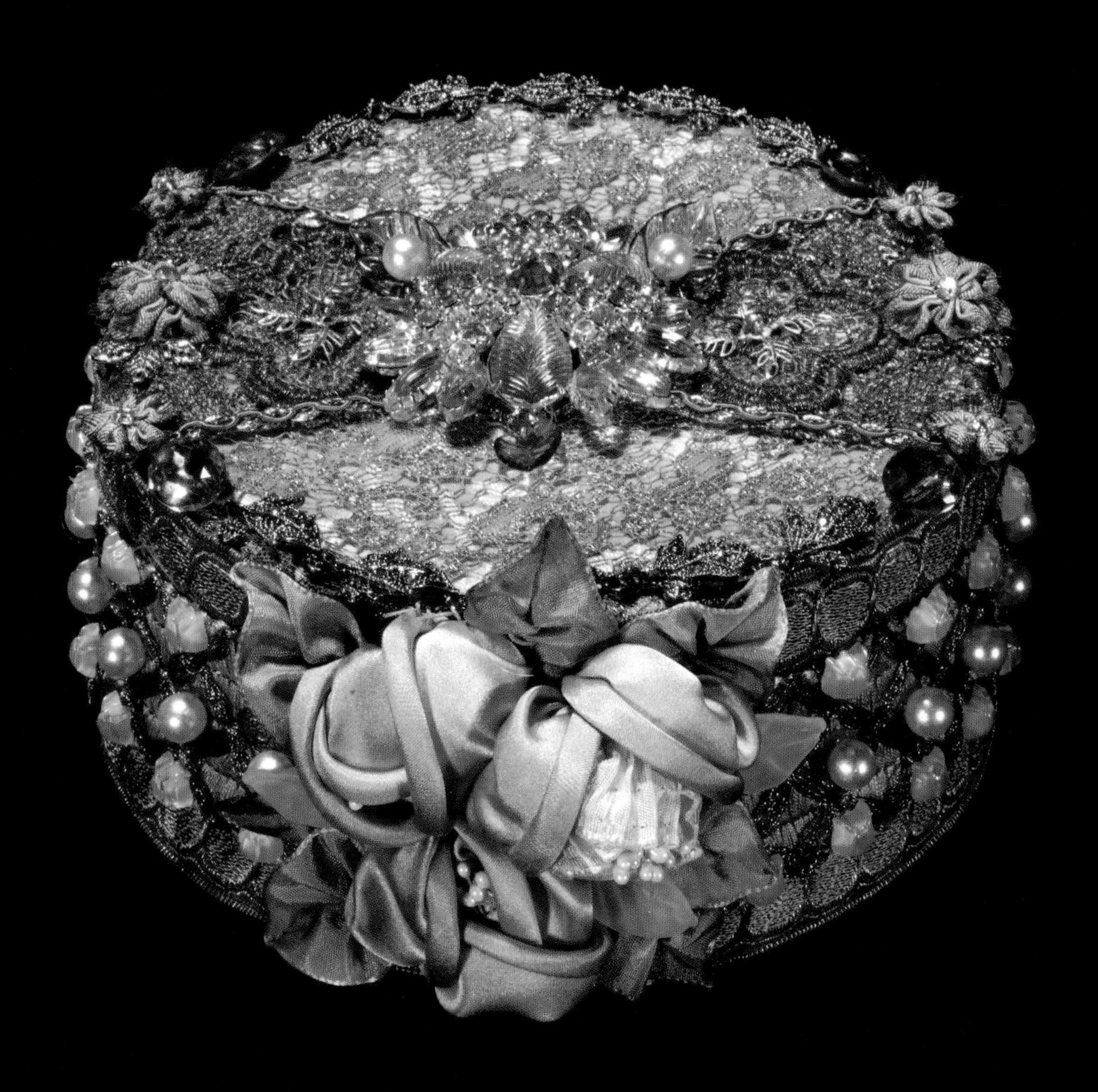

Plate 114

PLATE 115

Plate 116

Plate 117

PLATE 118

PLATE 119

Plate 120

PLATE 121

Plate 122

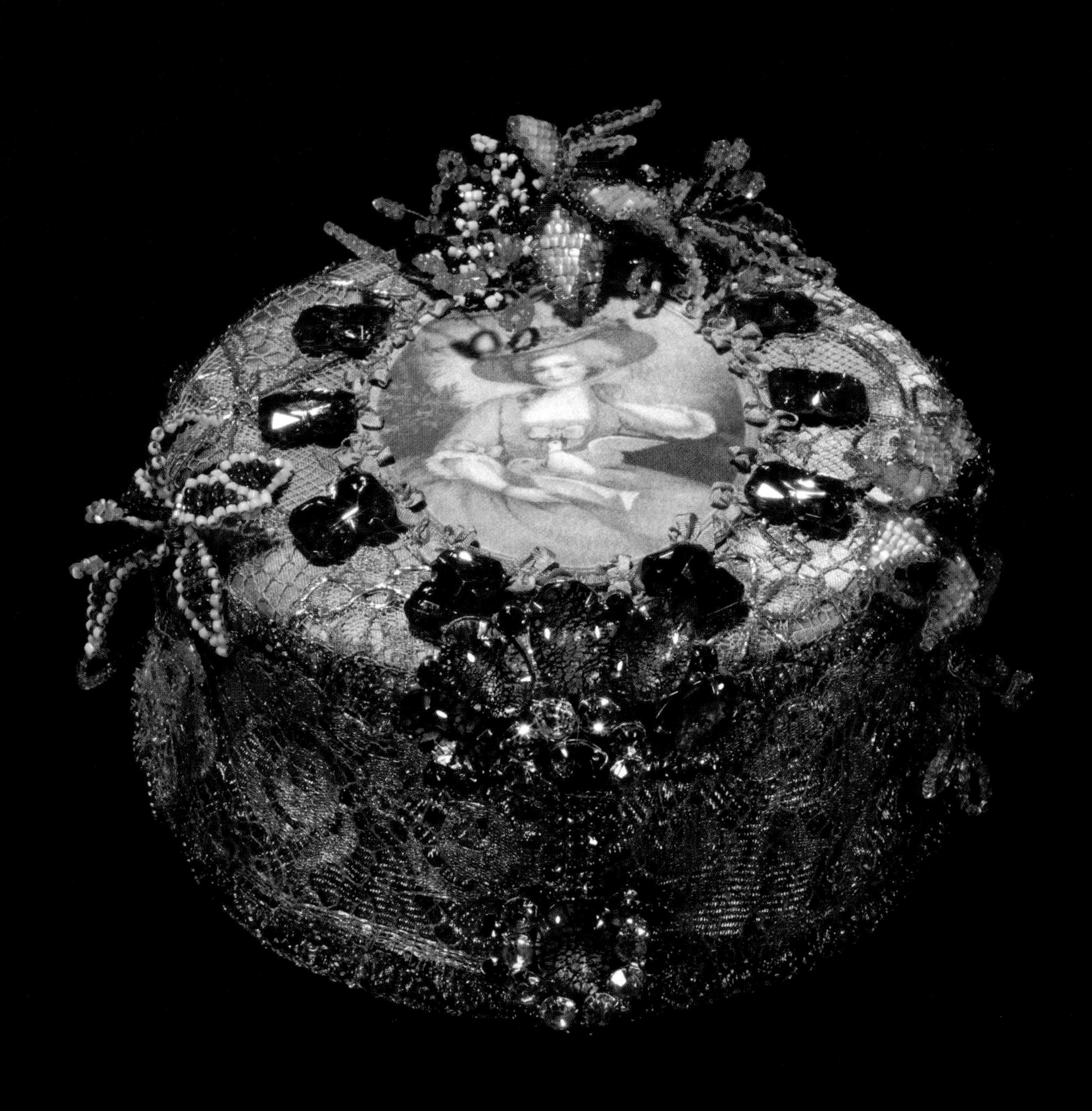

PLATE 123

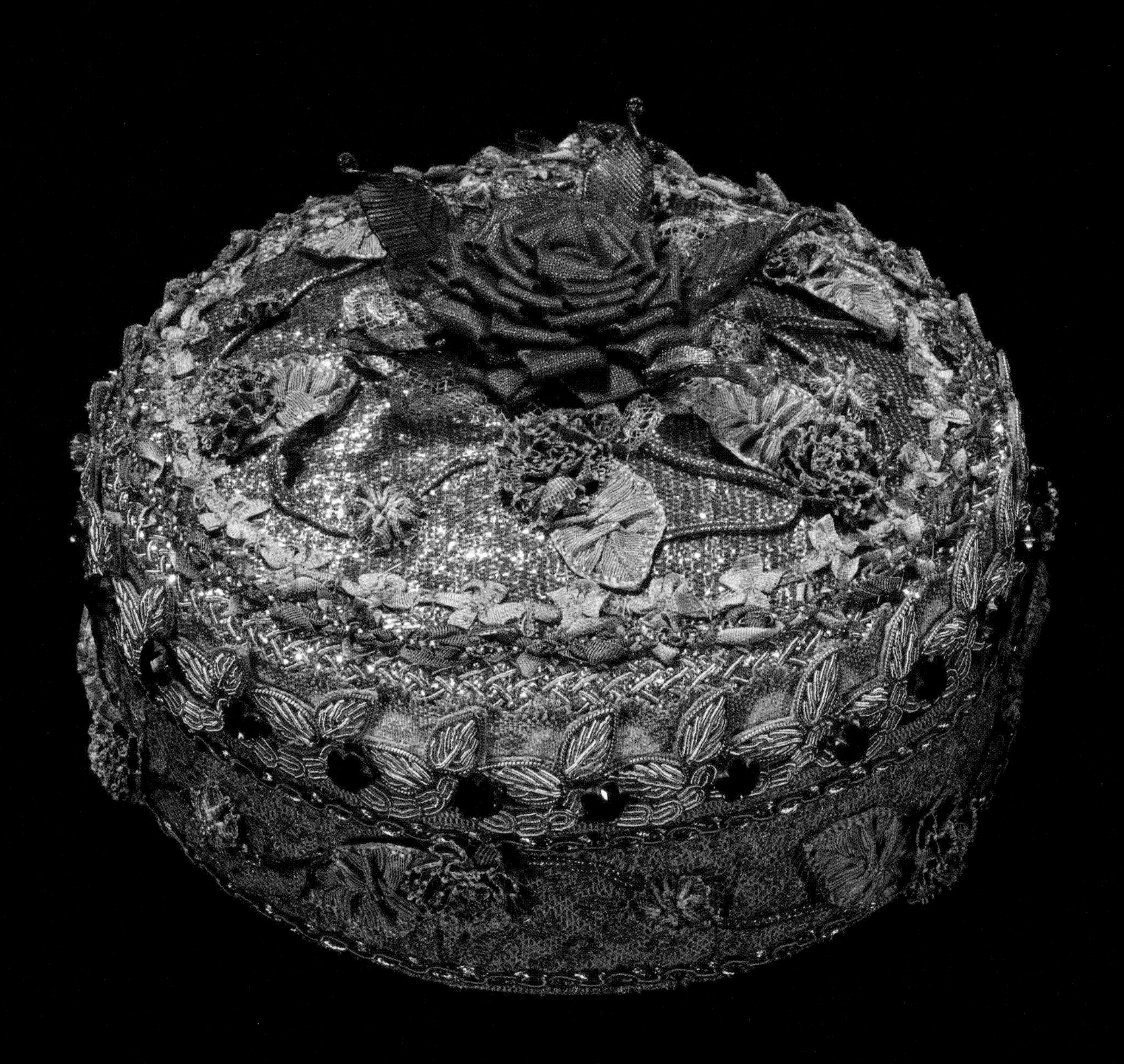

Plate 124

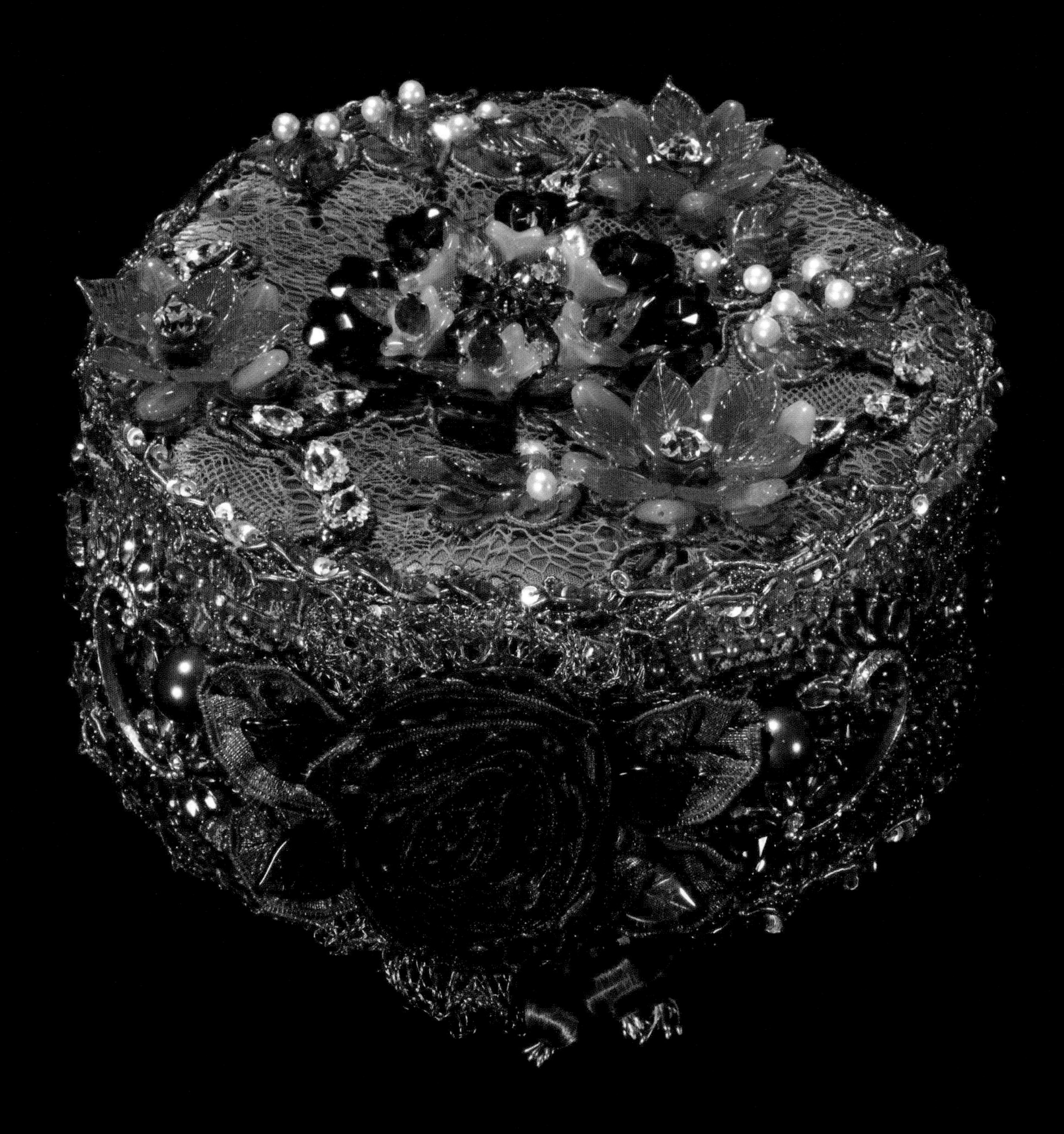

Plate 125

PLATE 126

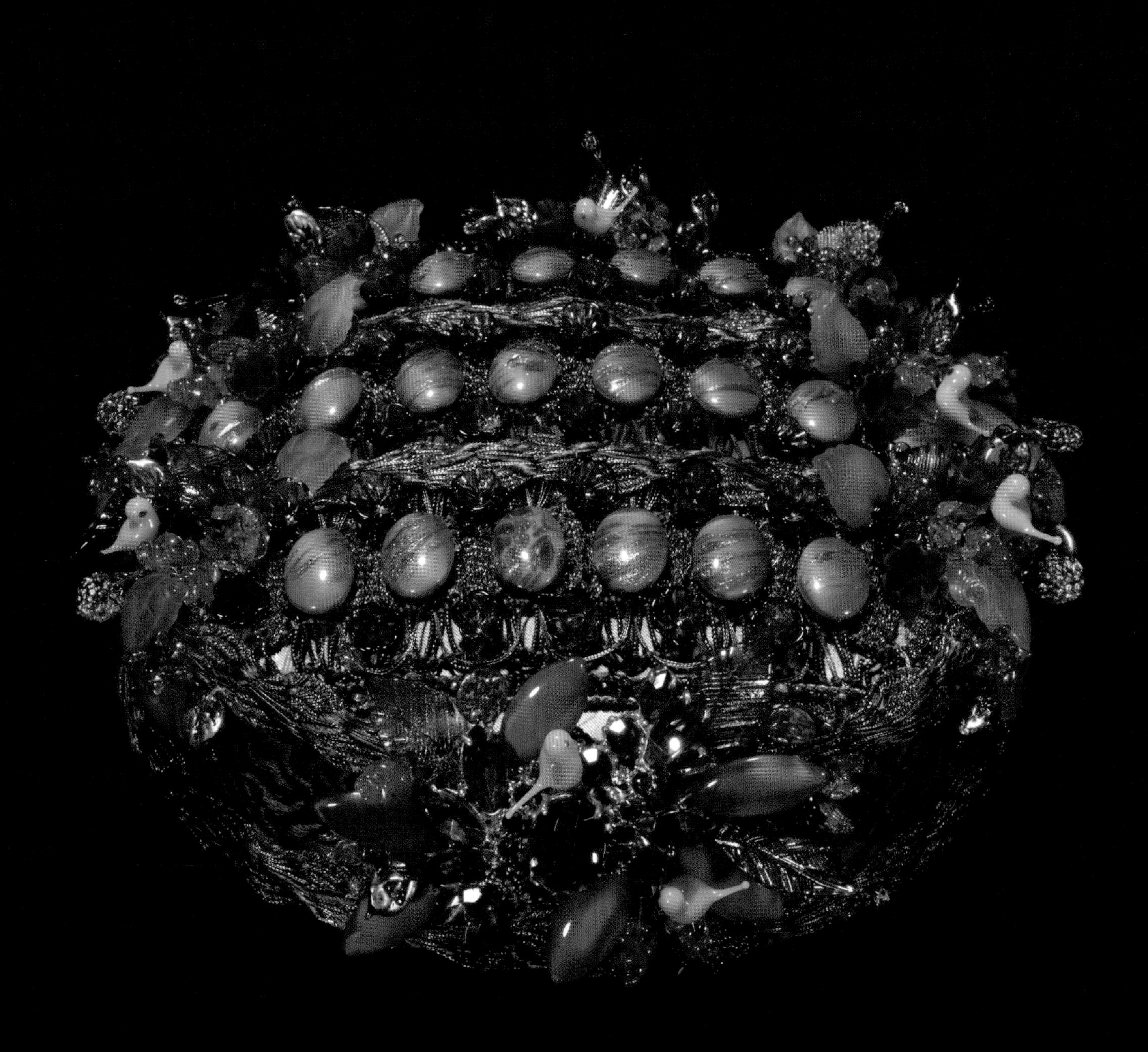

Plate 127

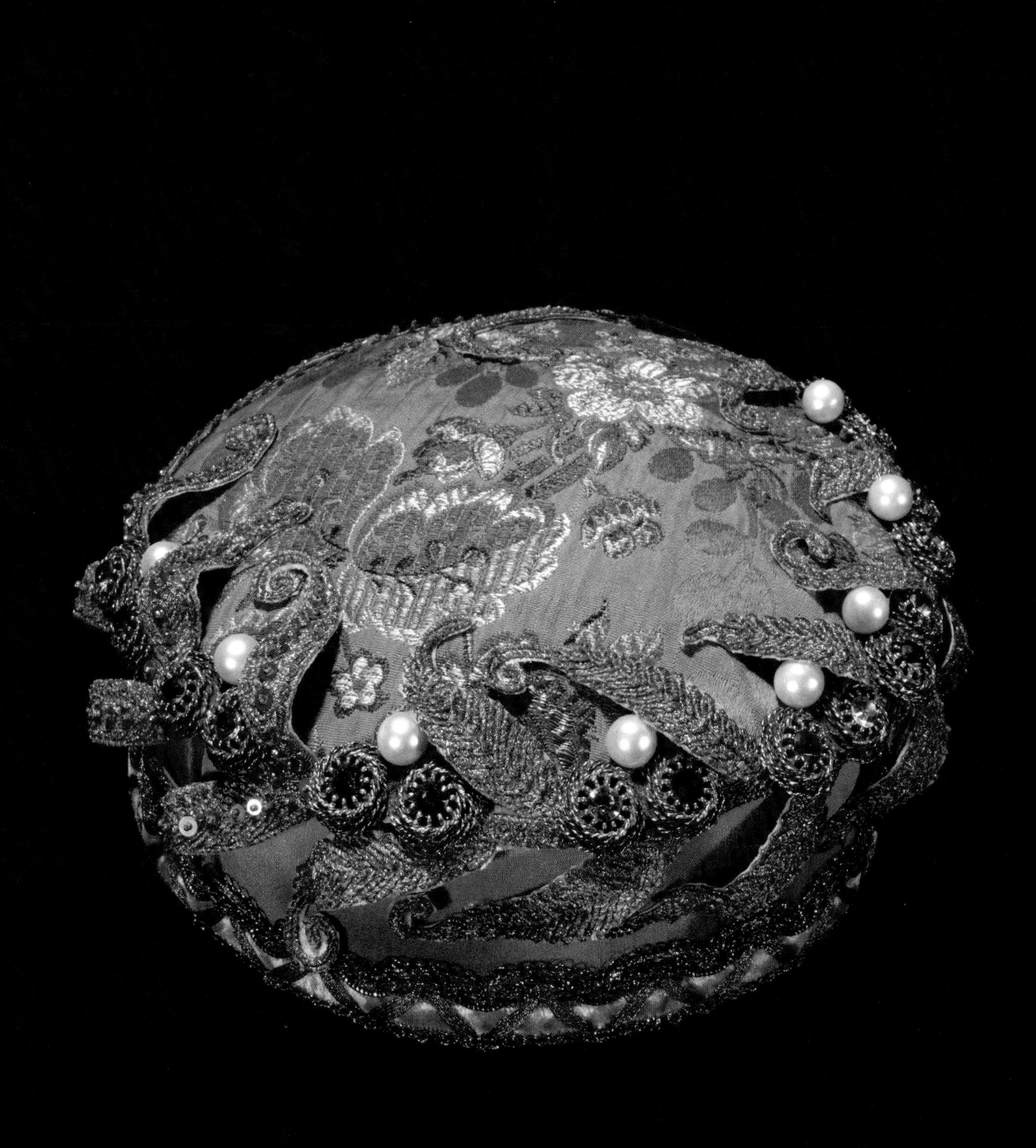

Plate 128

PLATE 129

Plate 130

PLATE 131

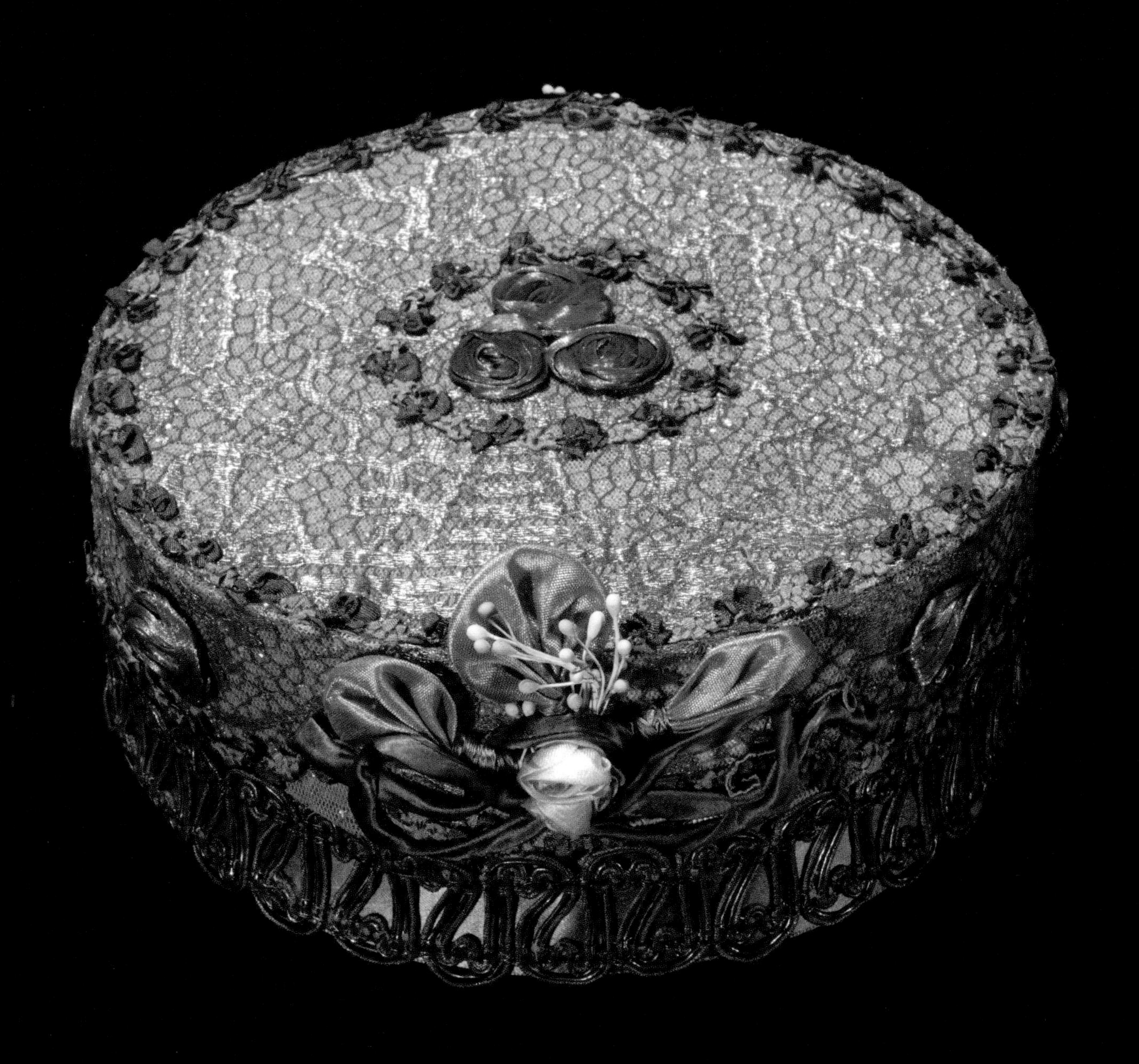

Plate 132

PLATE 133

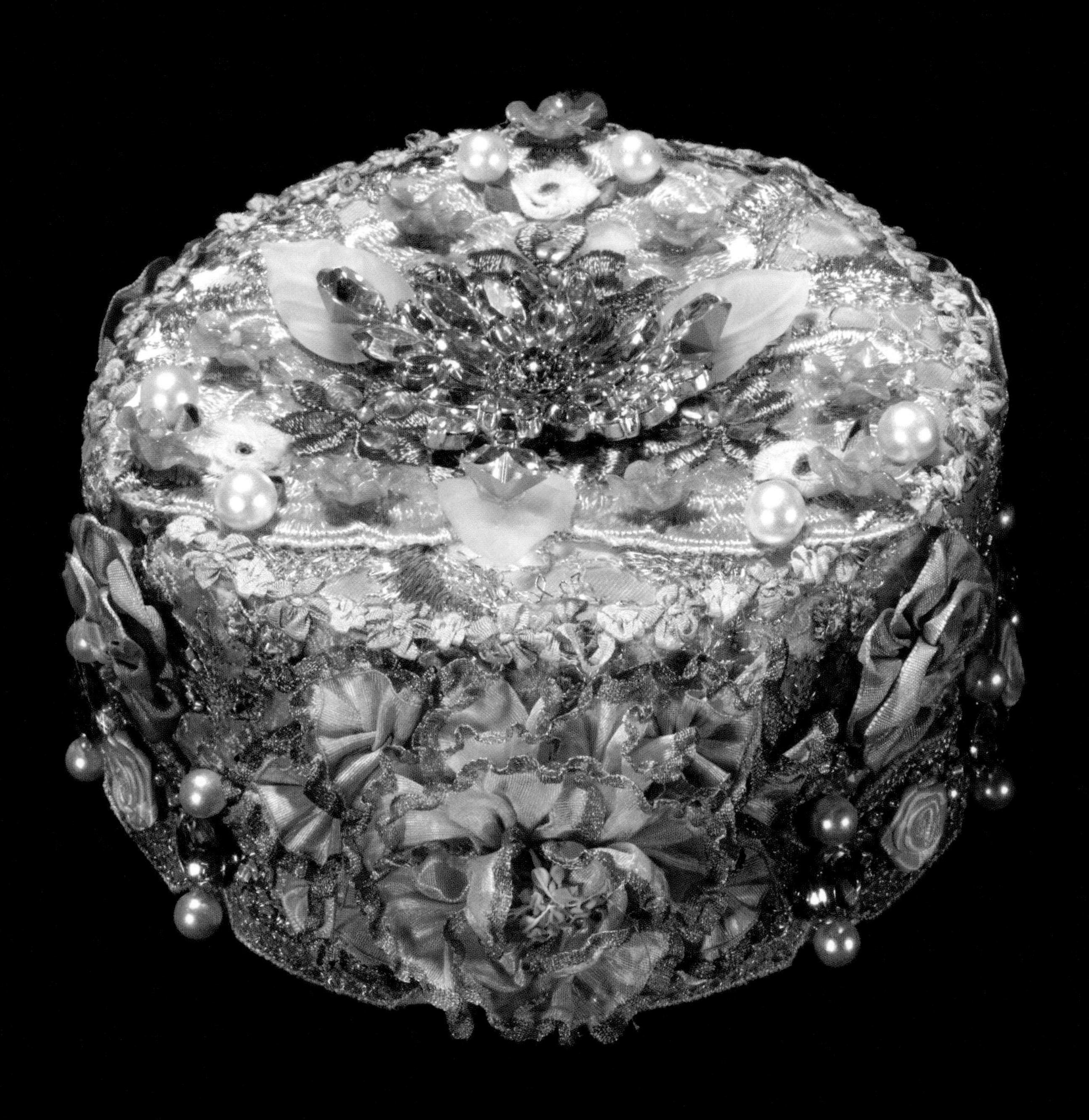

PLATE 134

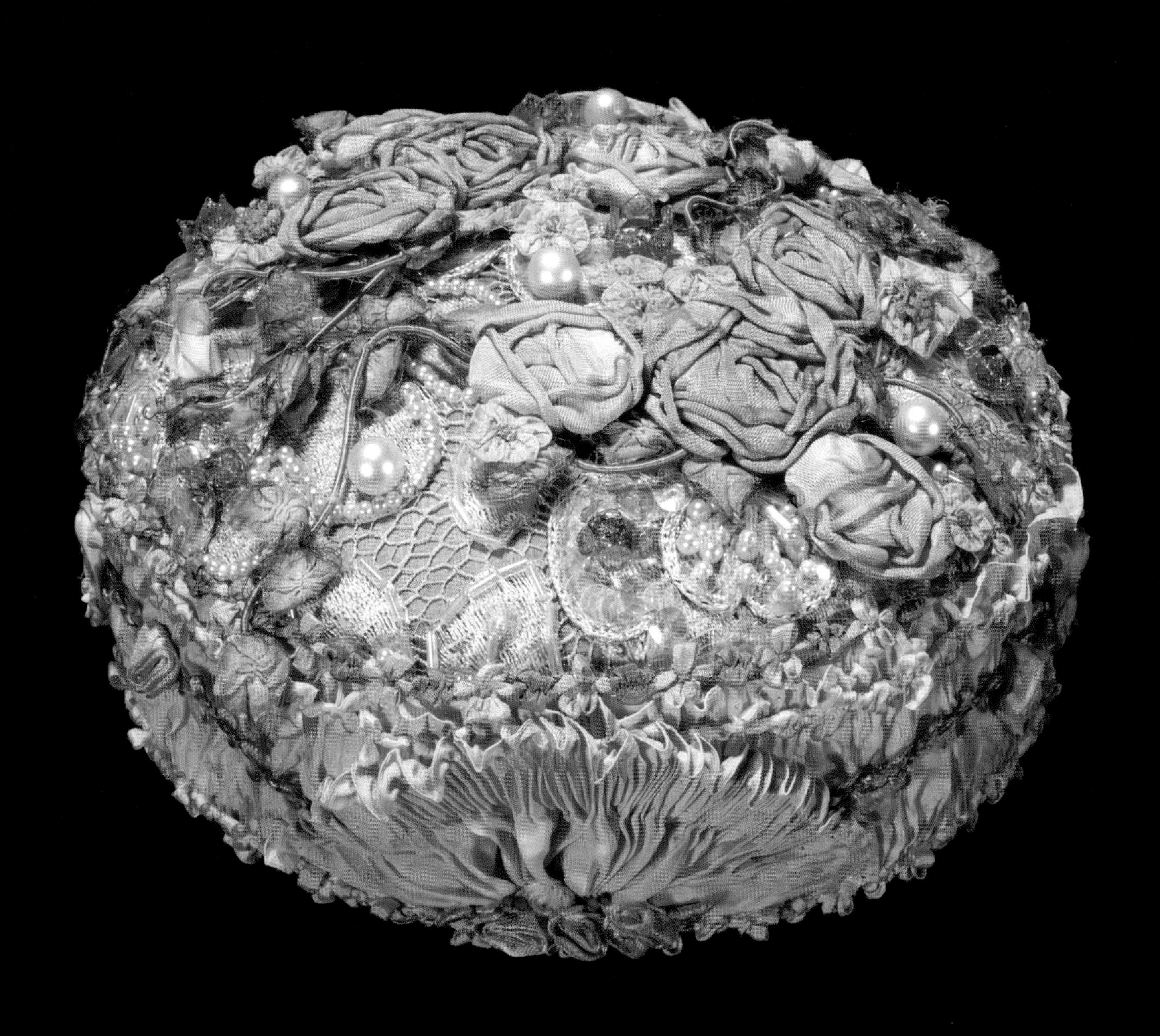

PLATE 135

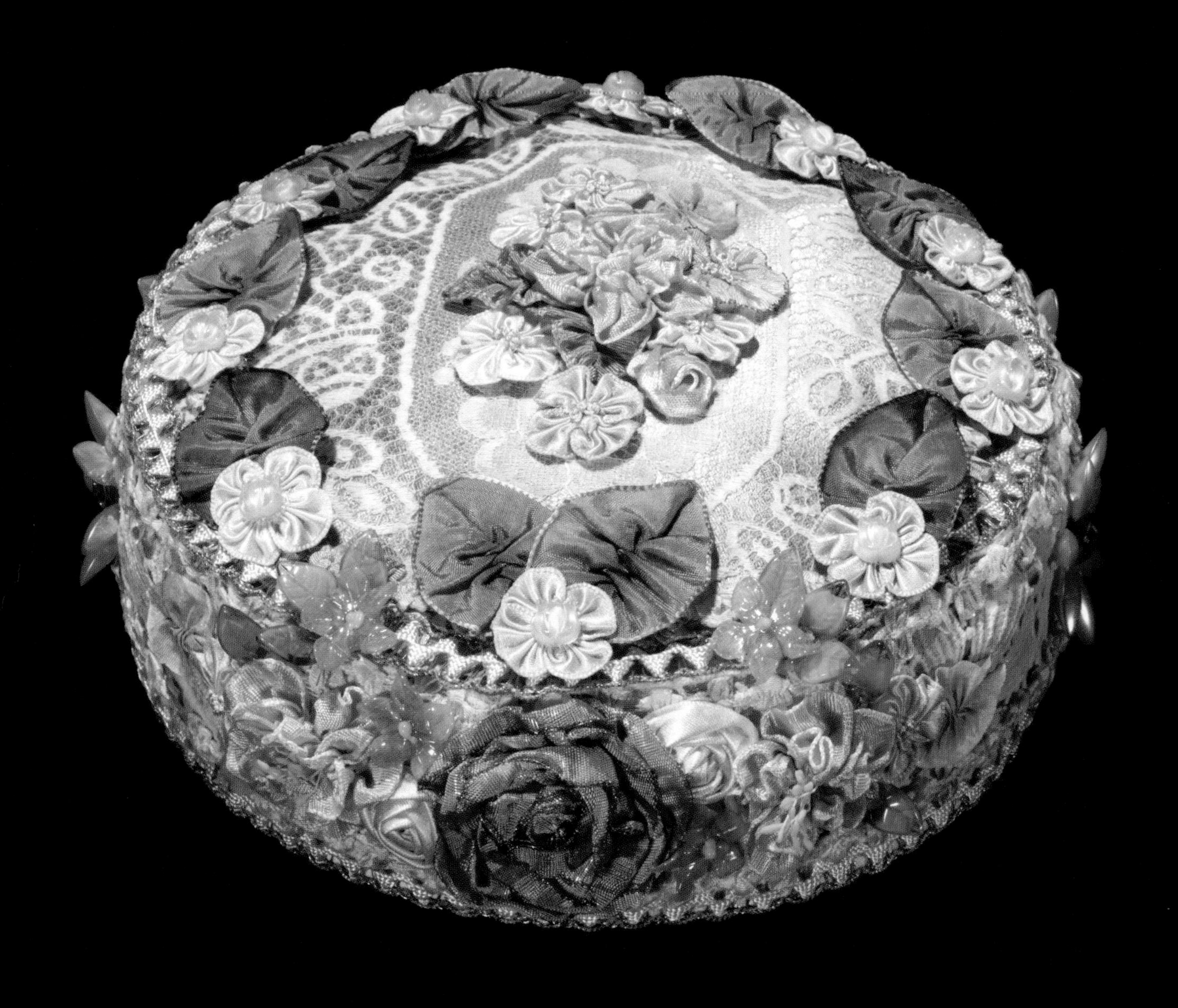

PLATE 136

PLATE 137

Plate 138

PLATE 139

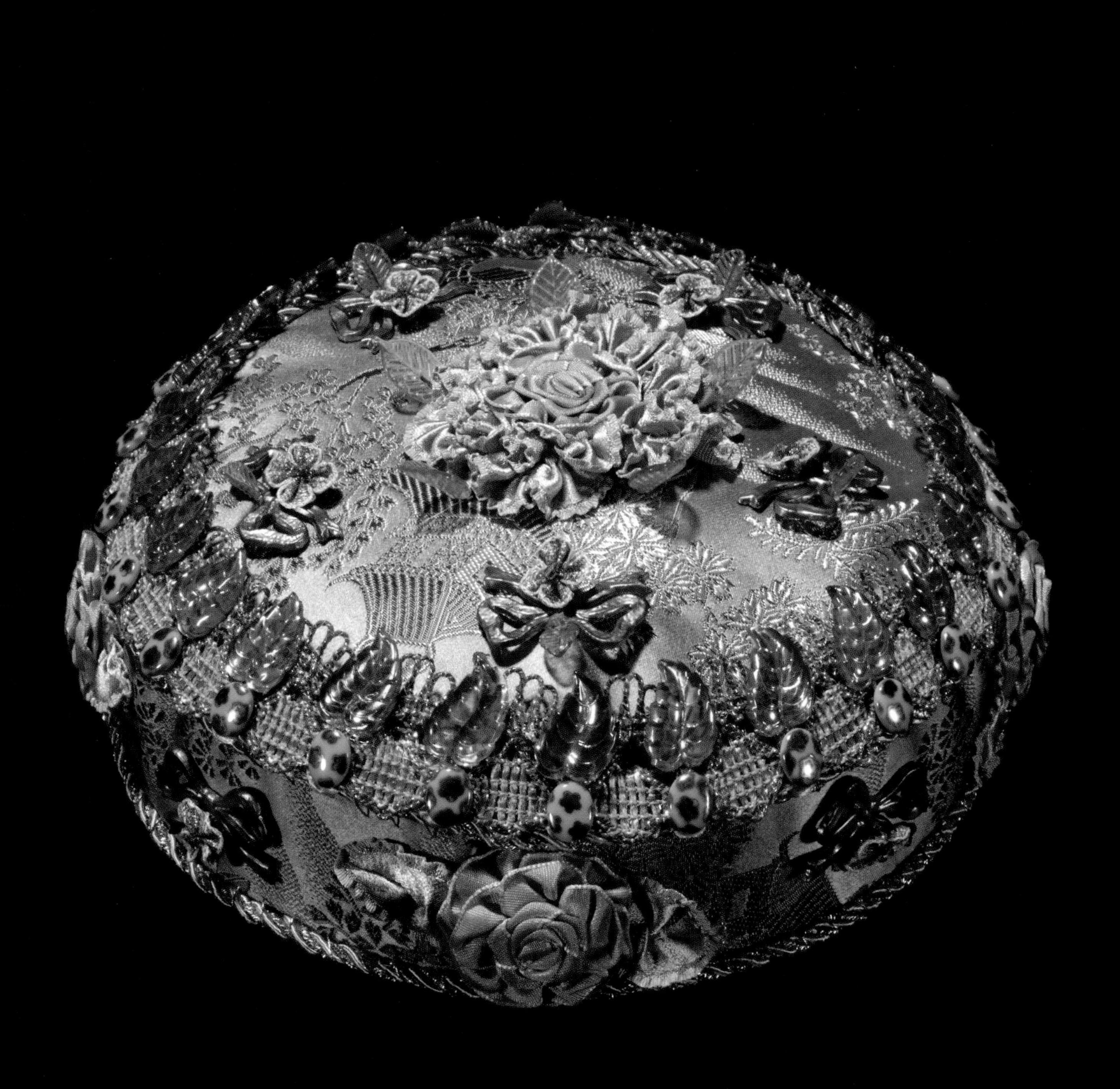

Plate 140

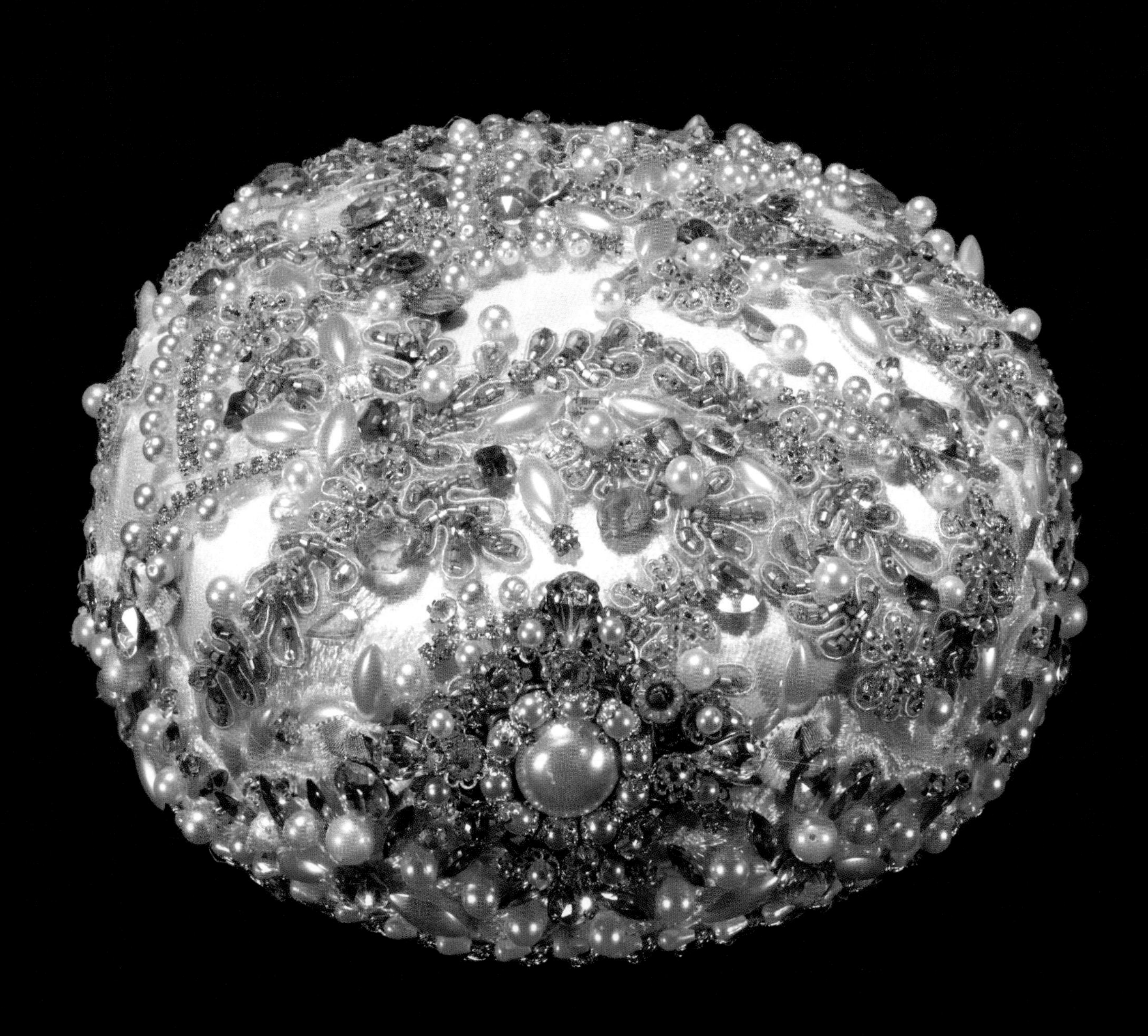

Plate 141

Plate 142

Plate 143

PLATE 144

PLATE 145

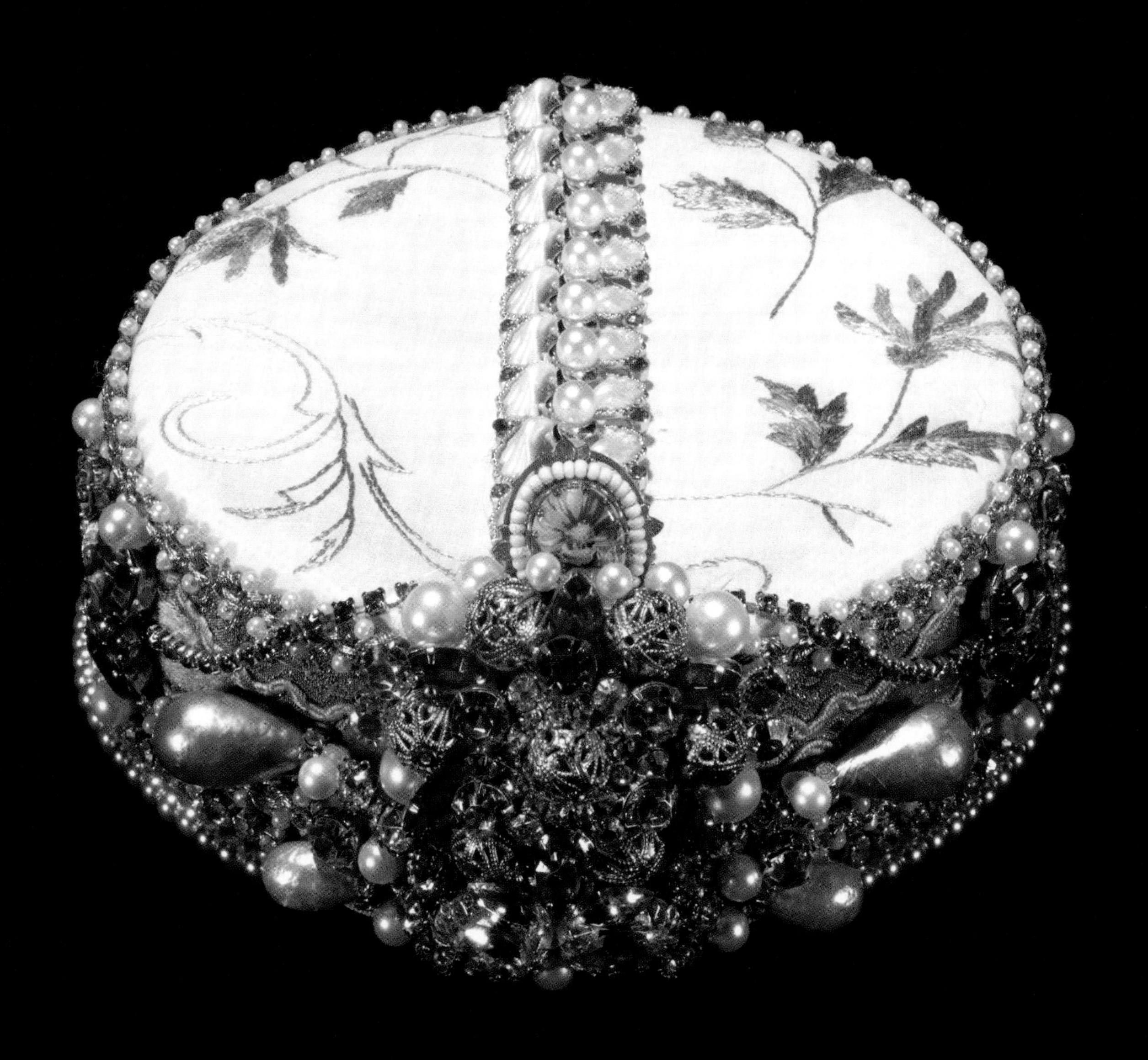

PLATE 146

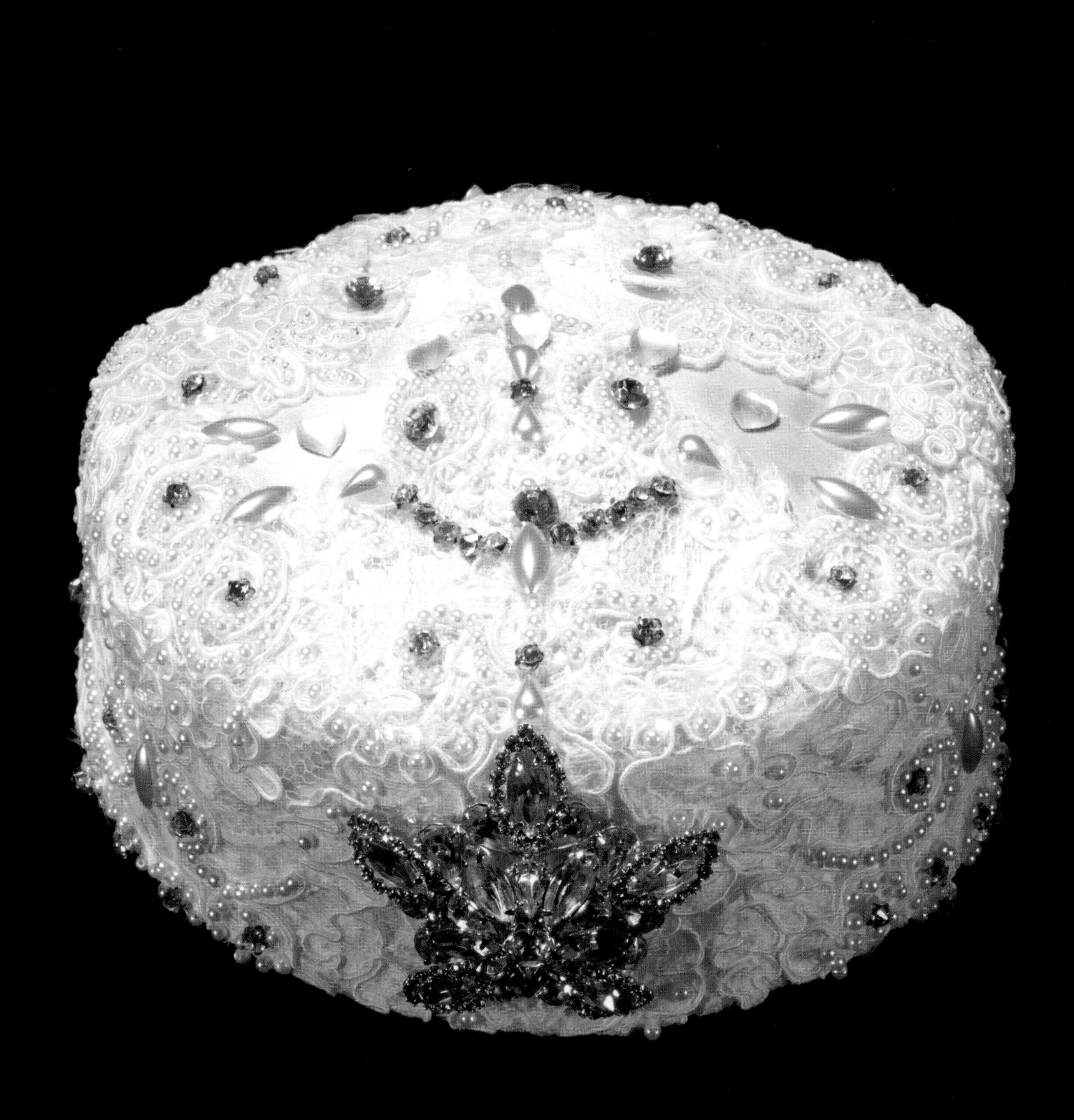

PLATE 147

PLATE 148

Plate 149

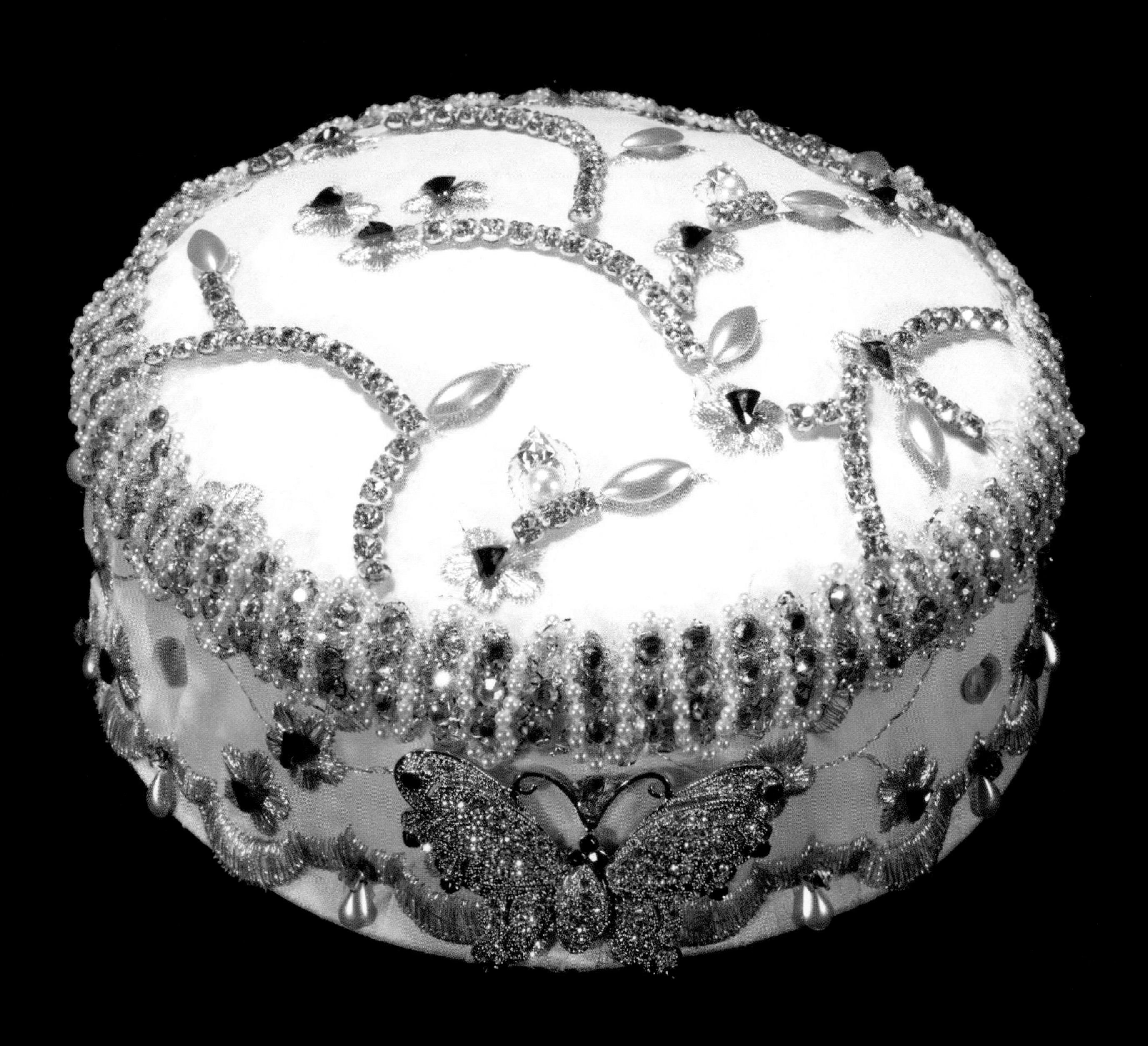

PLATE 150

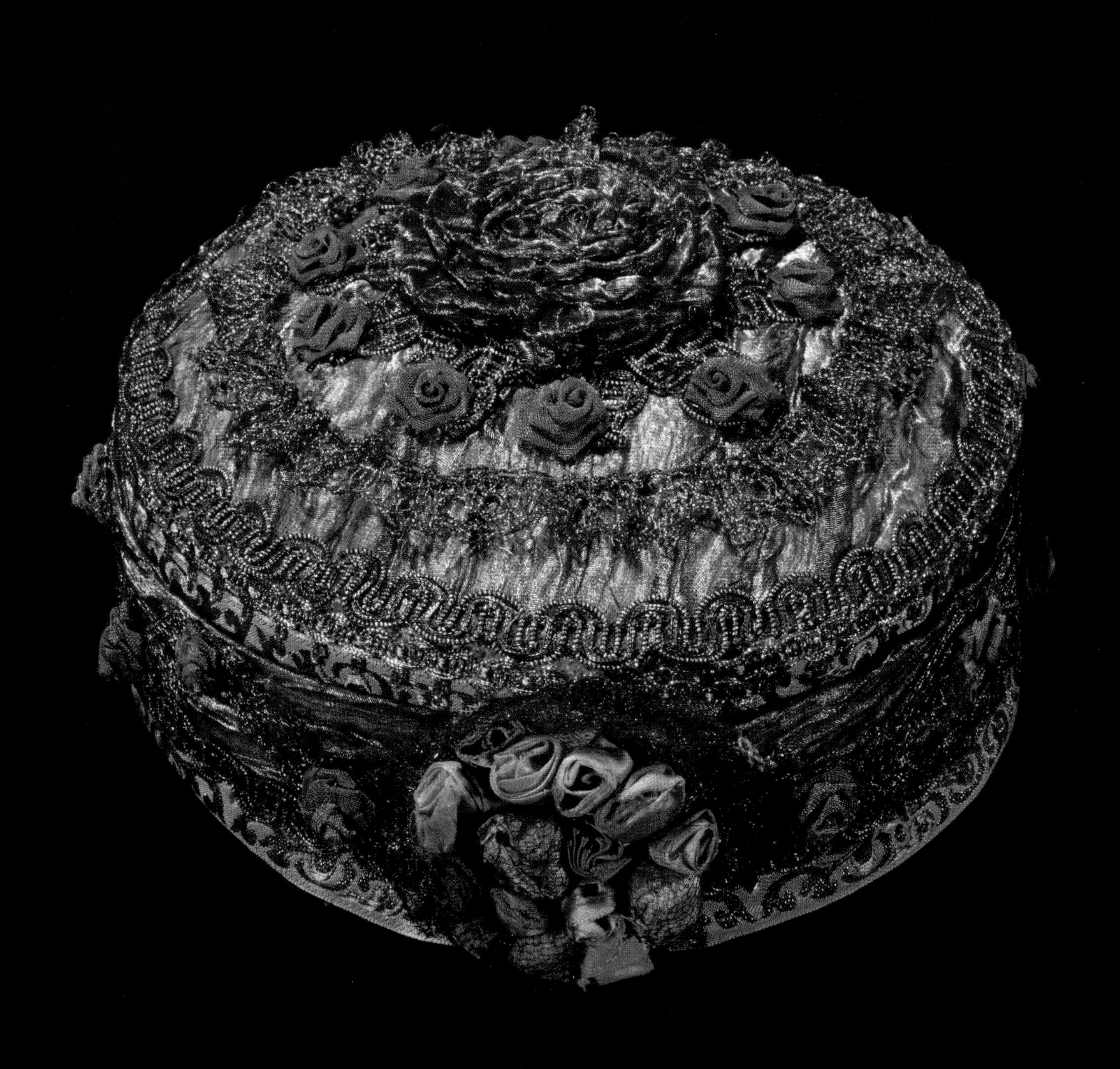

Plate 151

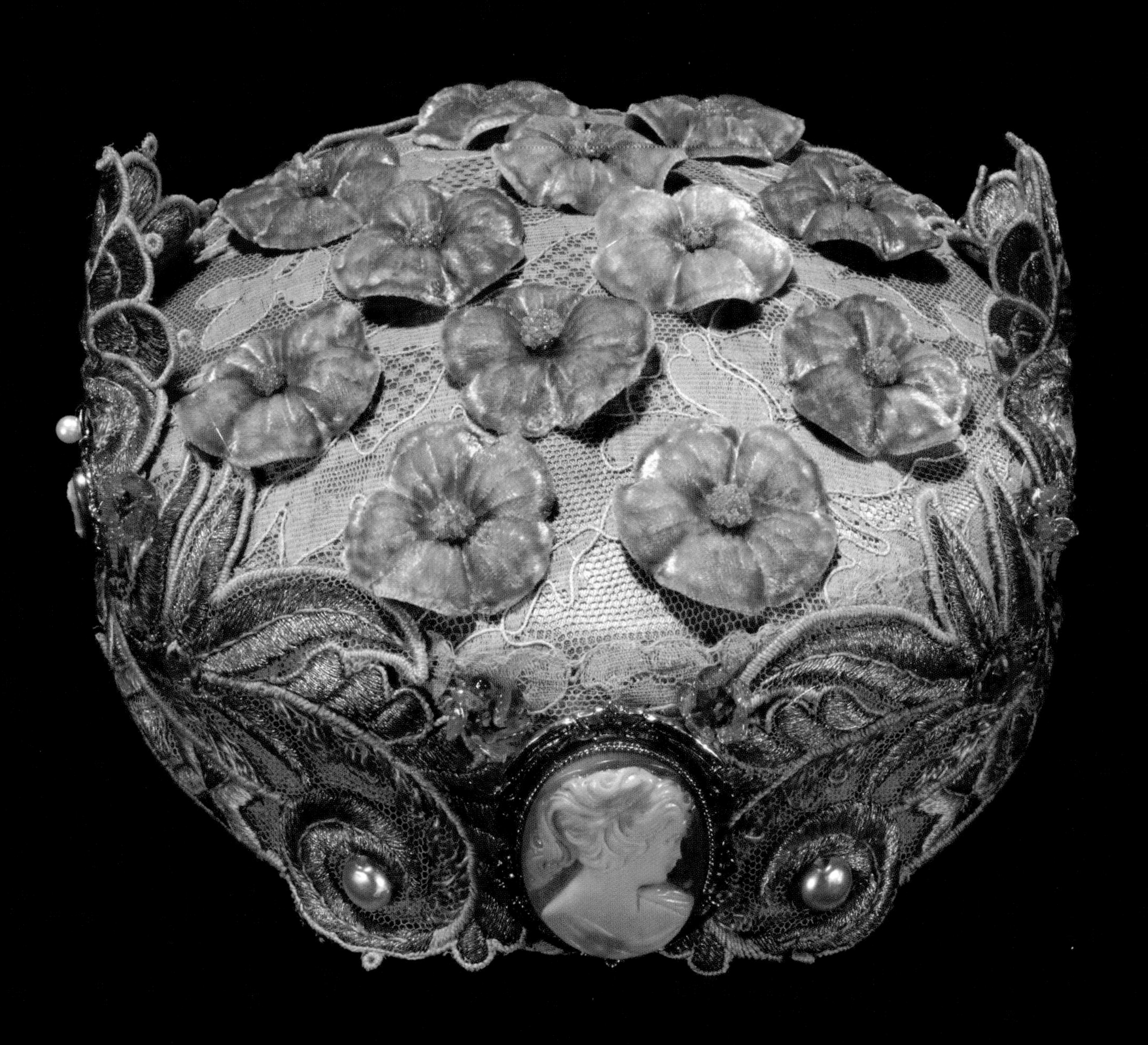

Plate 152

Plate 153

PLATE 154

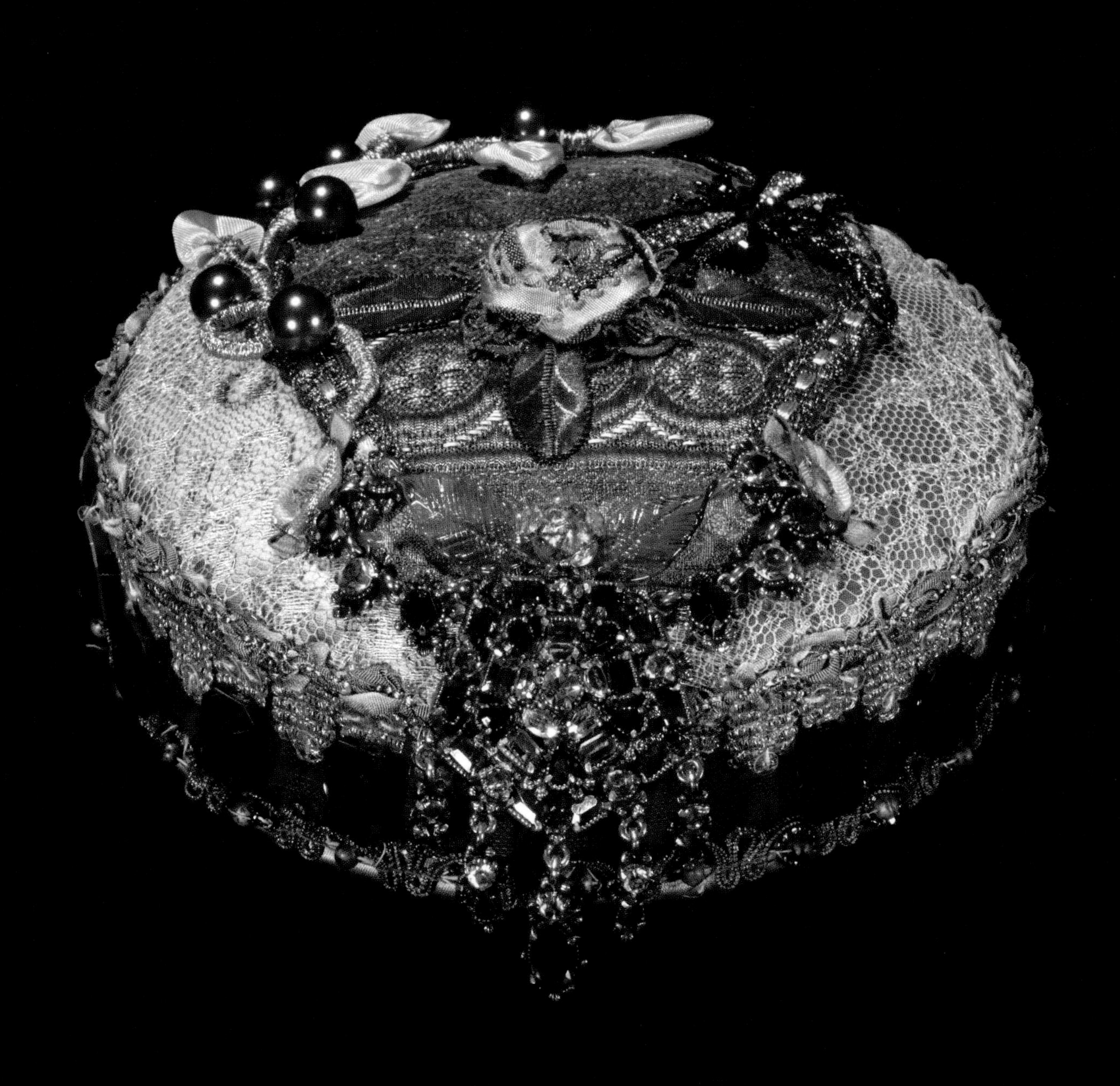

Plate 155

PLATE 156

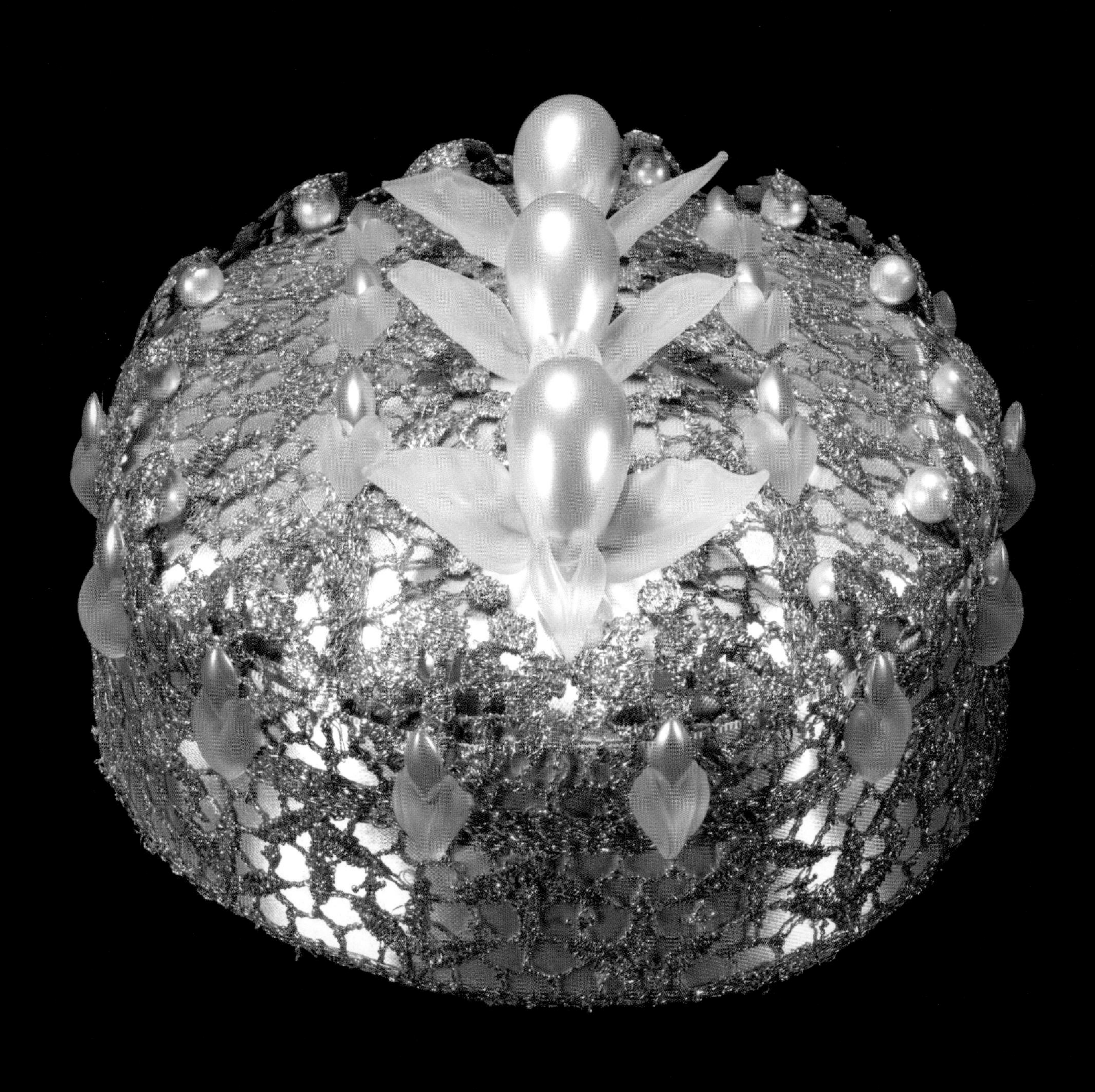

Plate 157

PLATE 158

PLATE 159

PLATE 160

Plate 161

Plate 162

Plate 163

PLATE 164

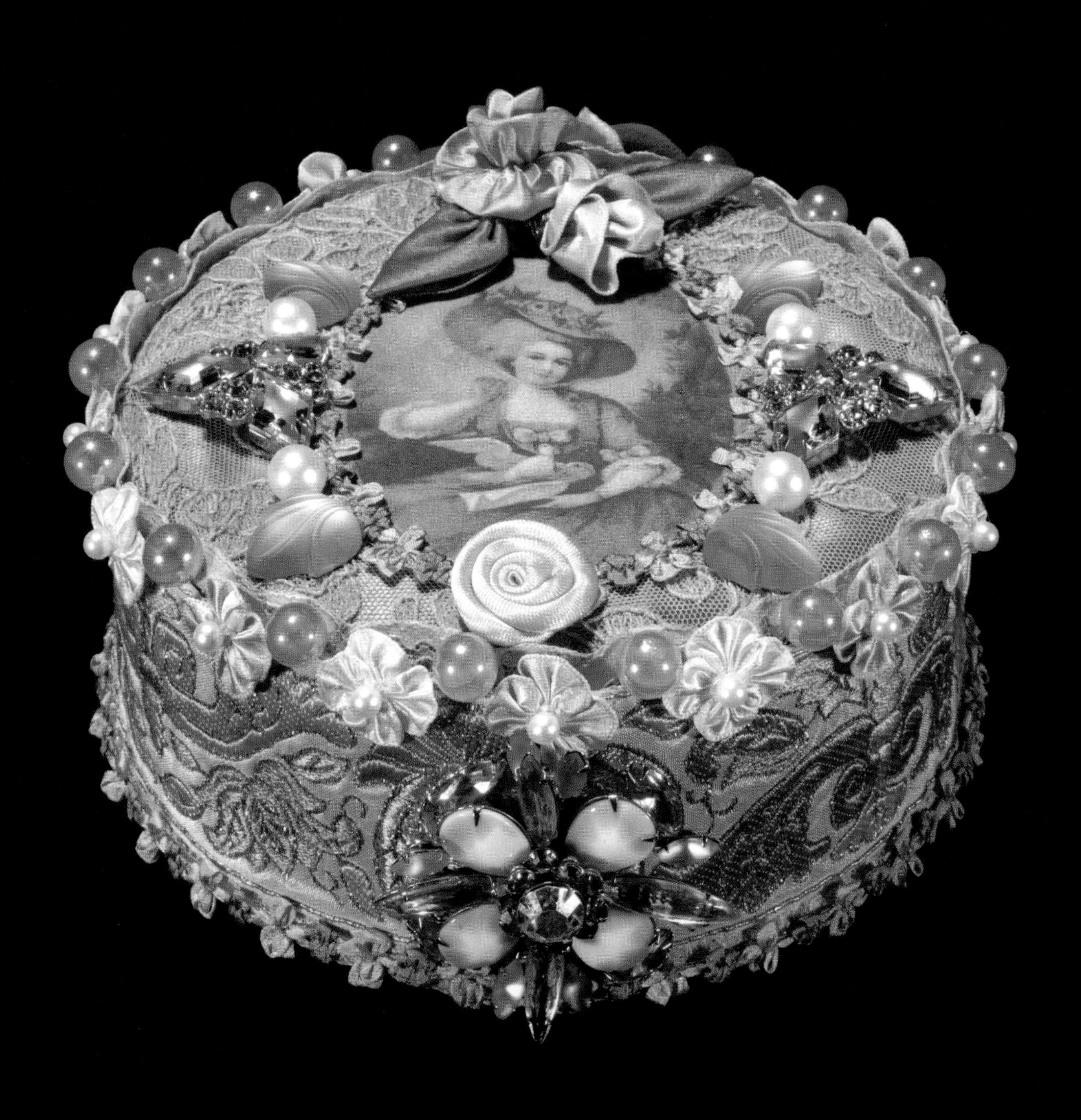

Plate 165

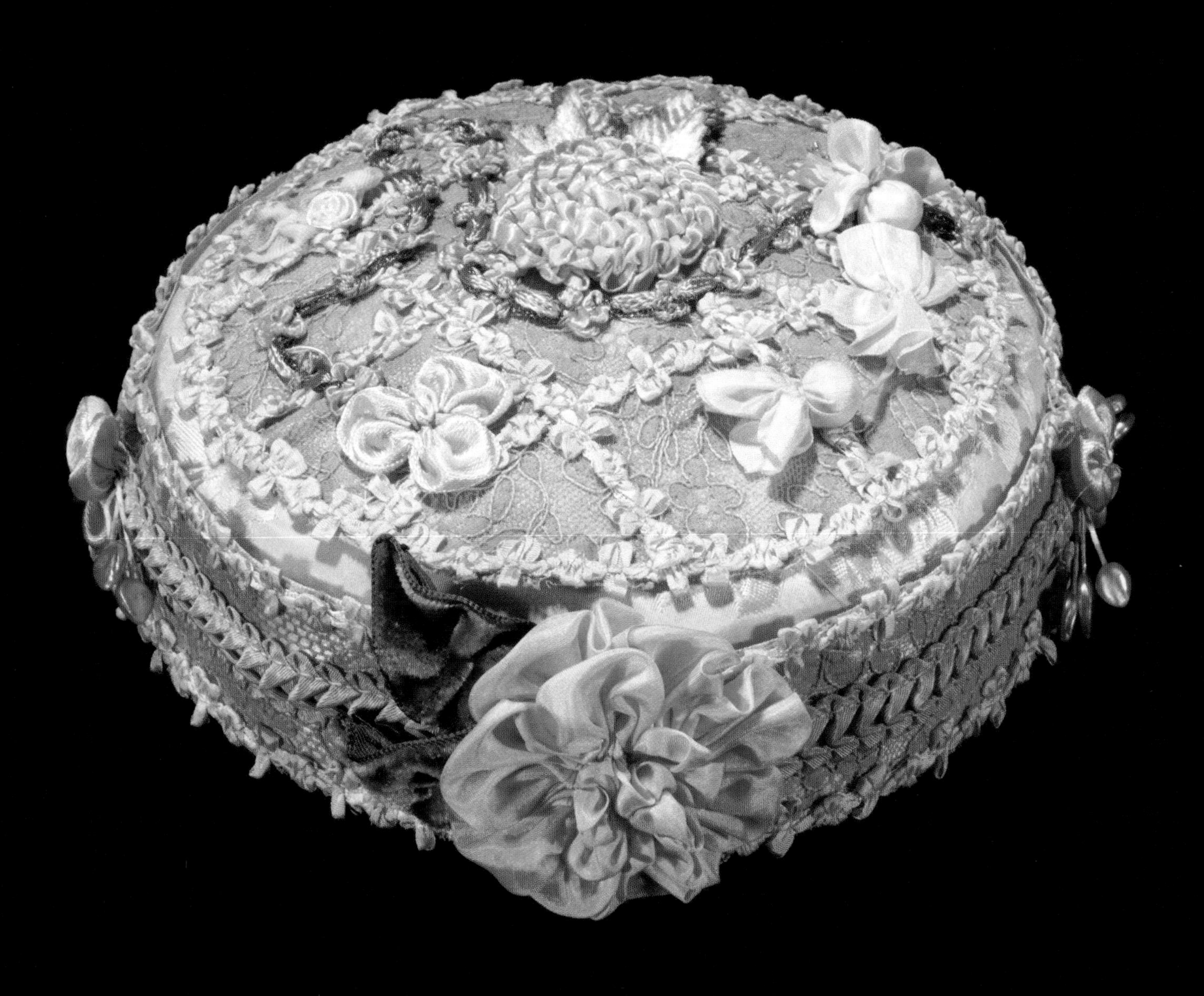

PLATE 166

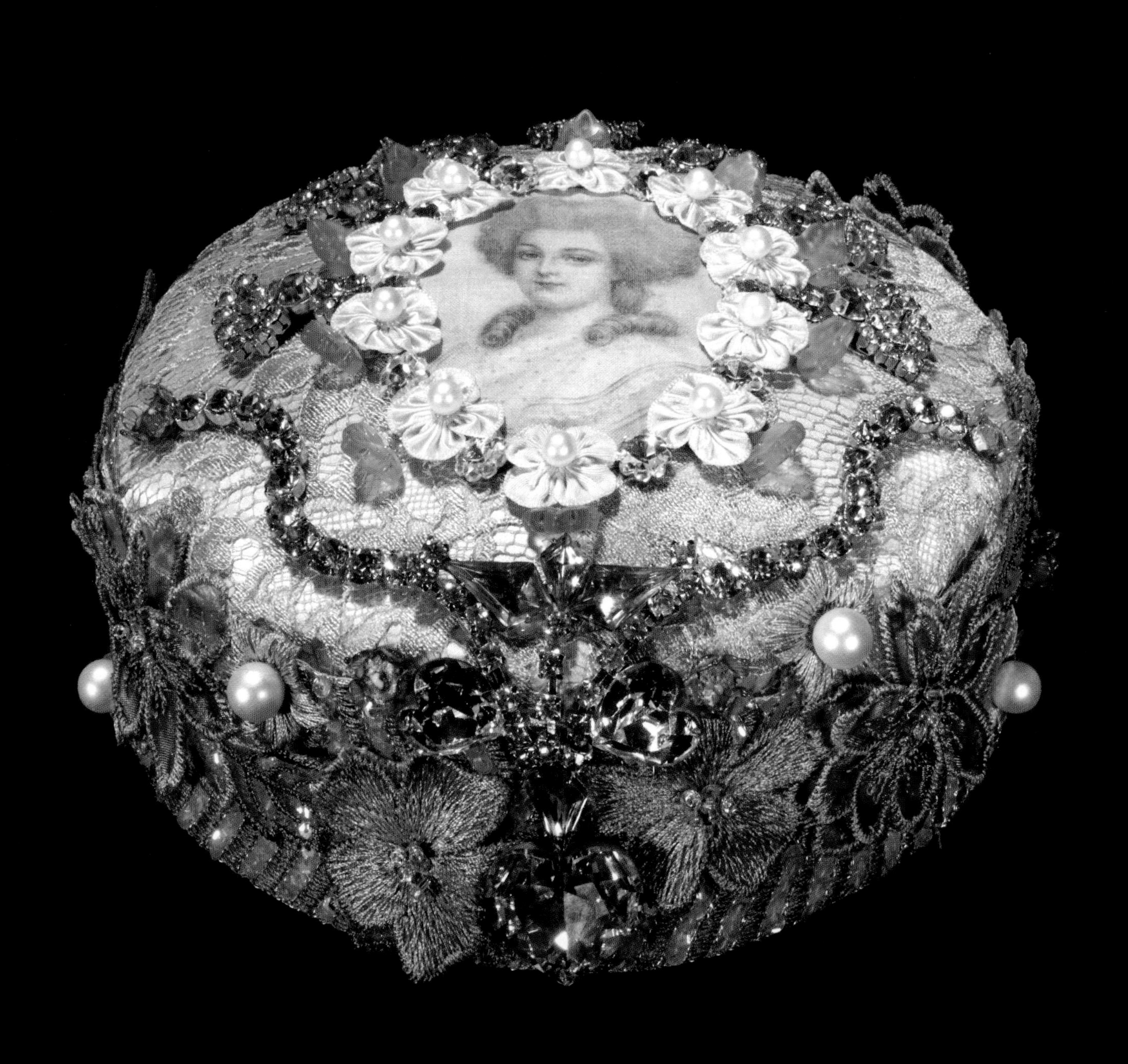

PLATE 167

PLATE 168

Plate 169

Plate 170

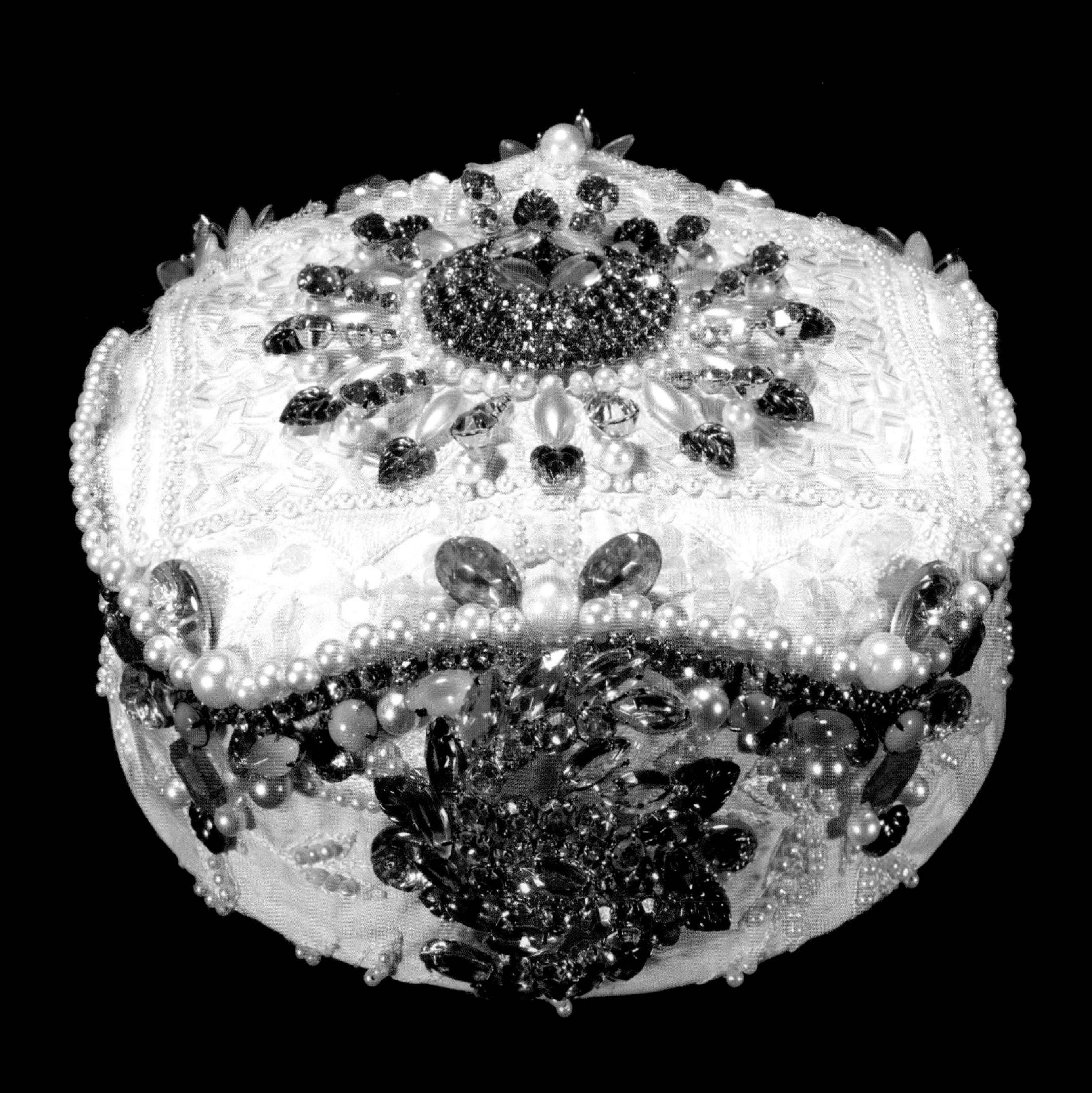

PLATE 171

PLATE 172

PLATE 173

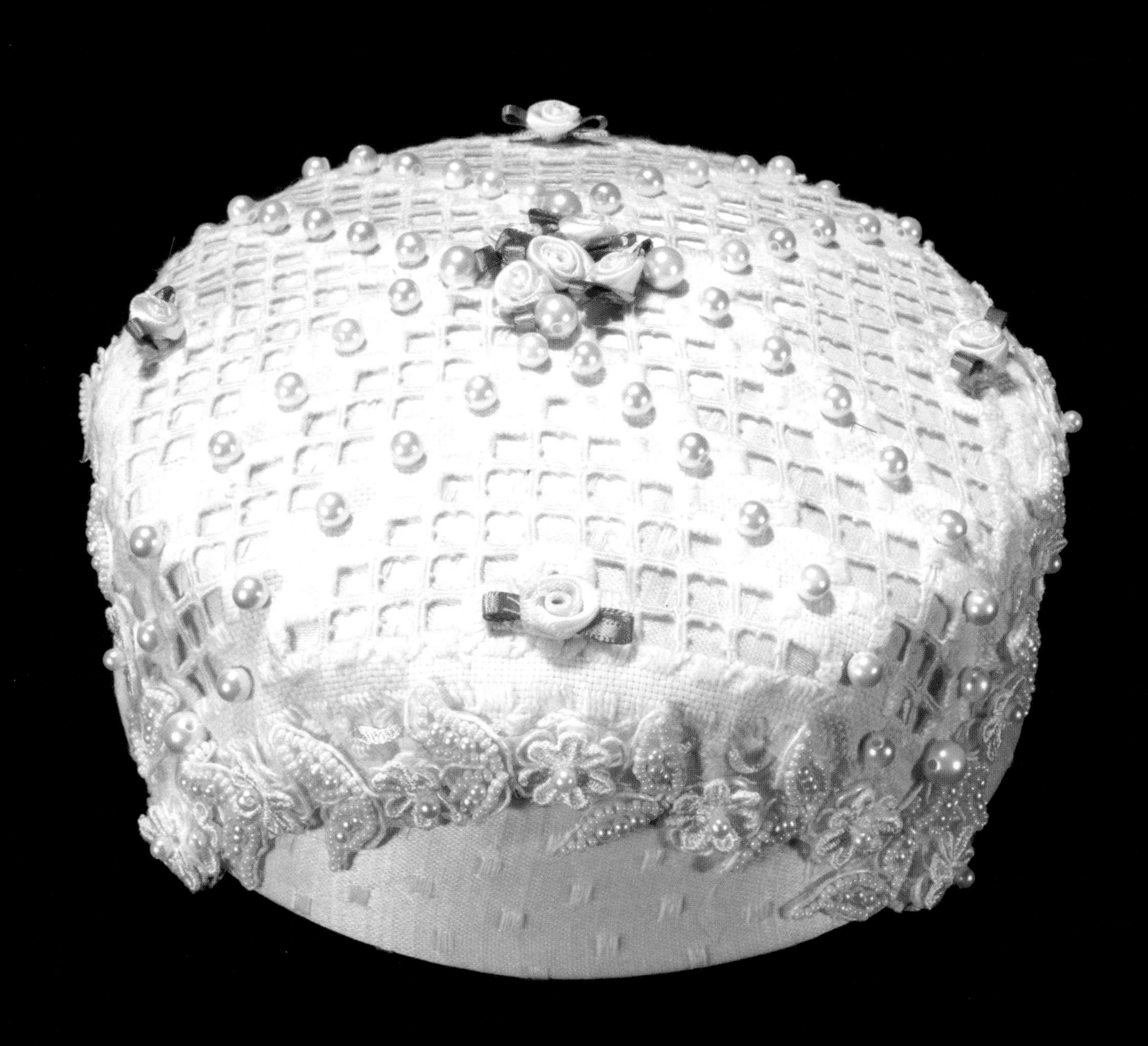

Plate 174

Plate 175

PLATE 176

Plate 177

PLATE 178

PLATE 179

Plate 180

PLATE 181

Plate 182

Plate 183

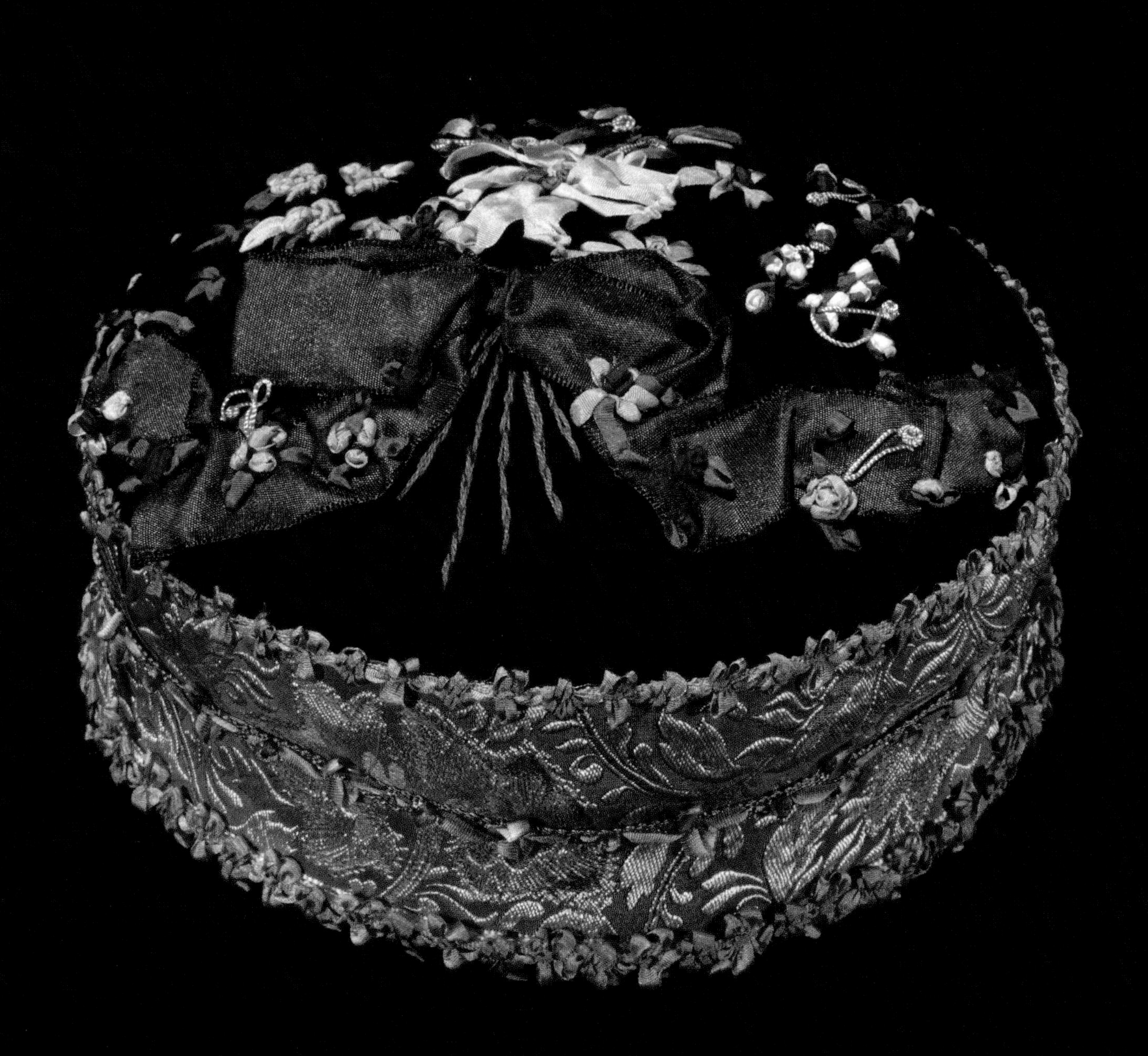

PLATE 184

PLATE 185

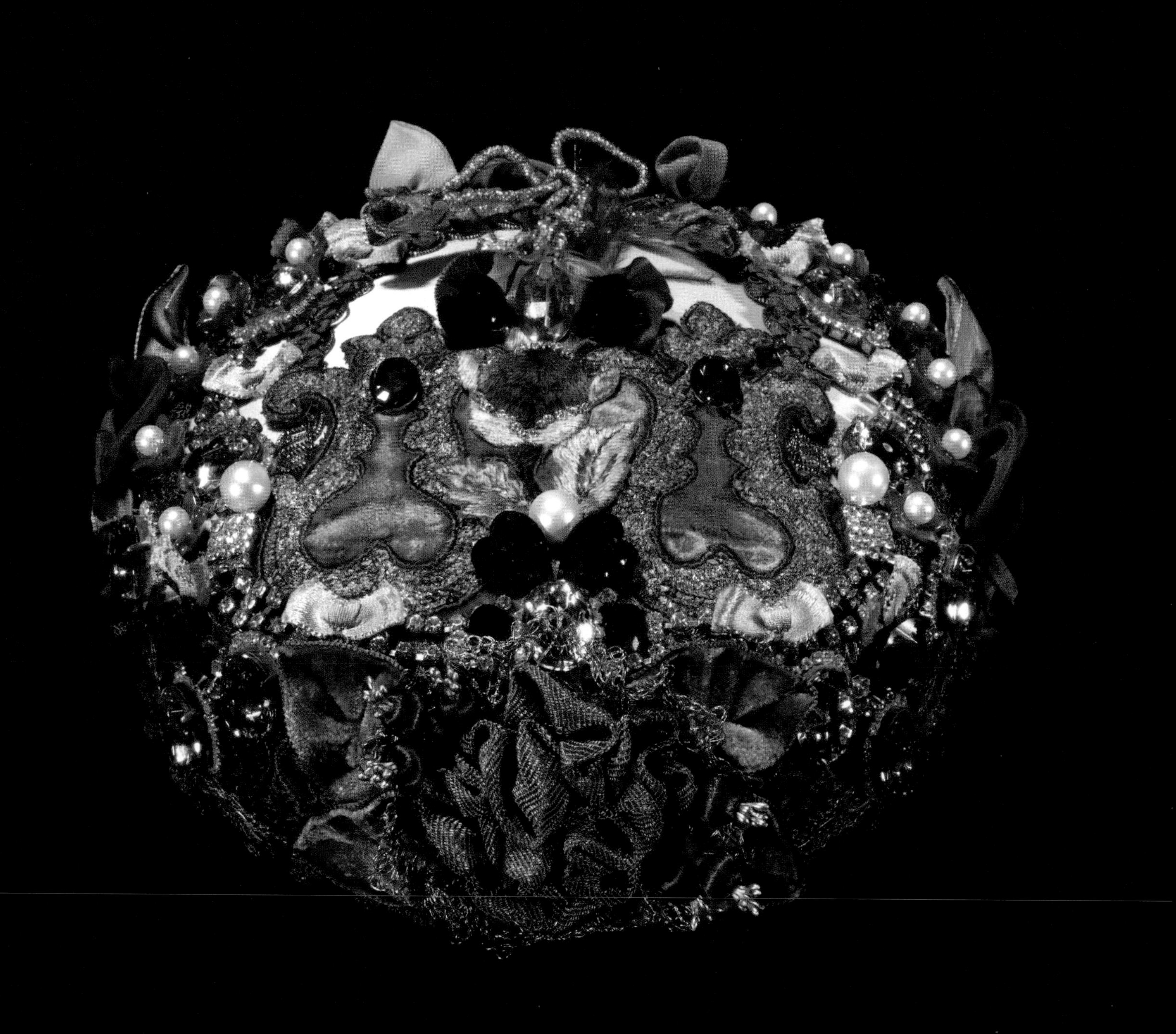

PLATE 186

PLATE 187

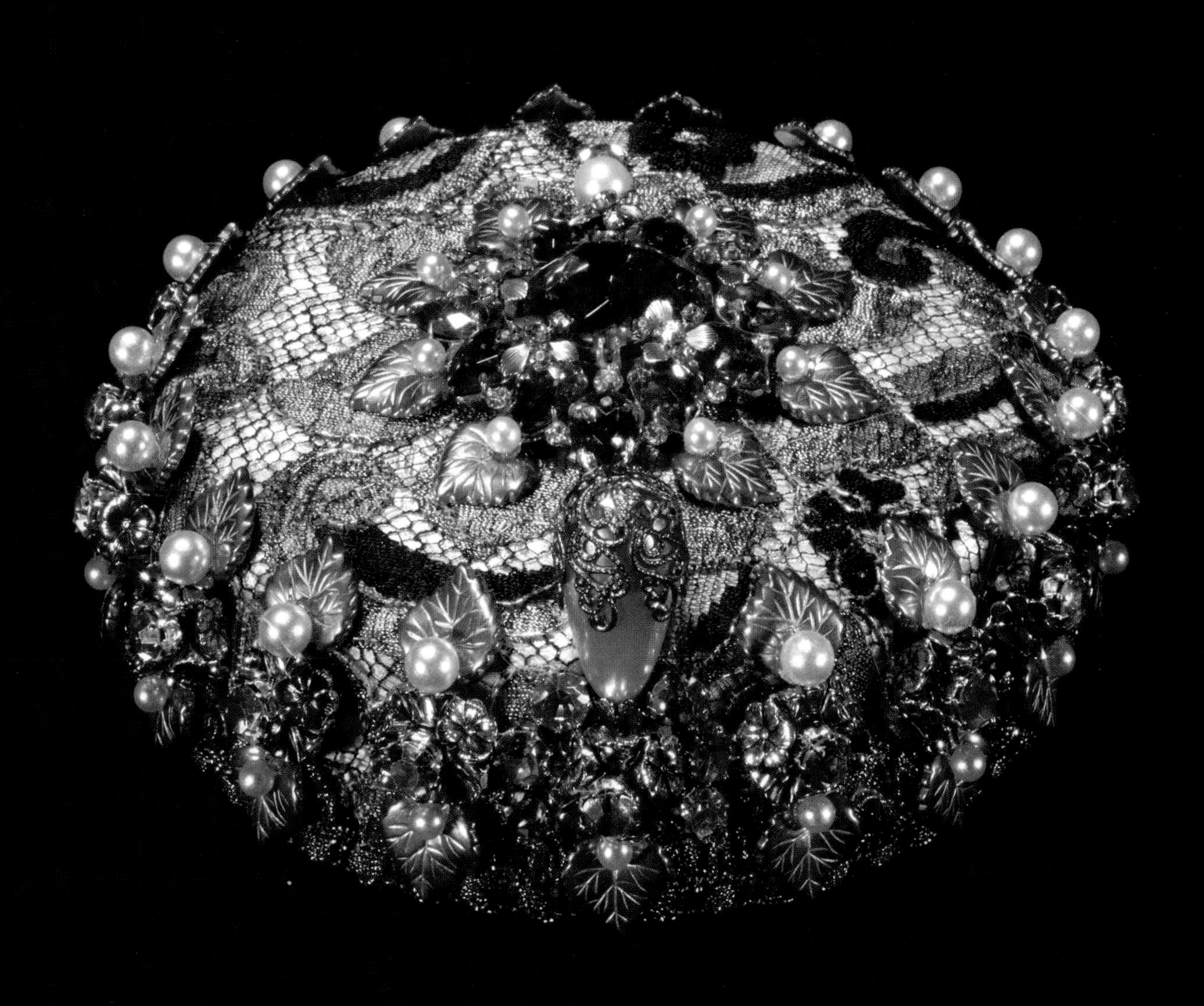

PLATE 188

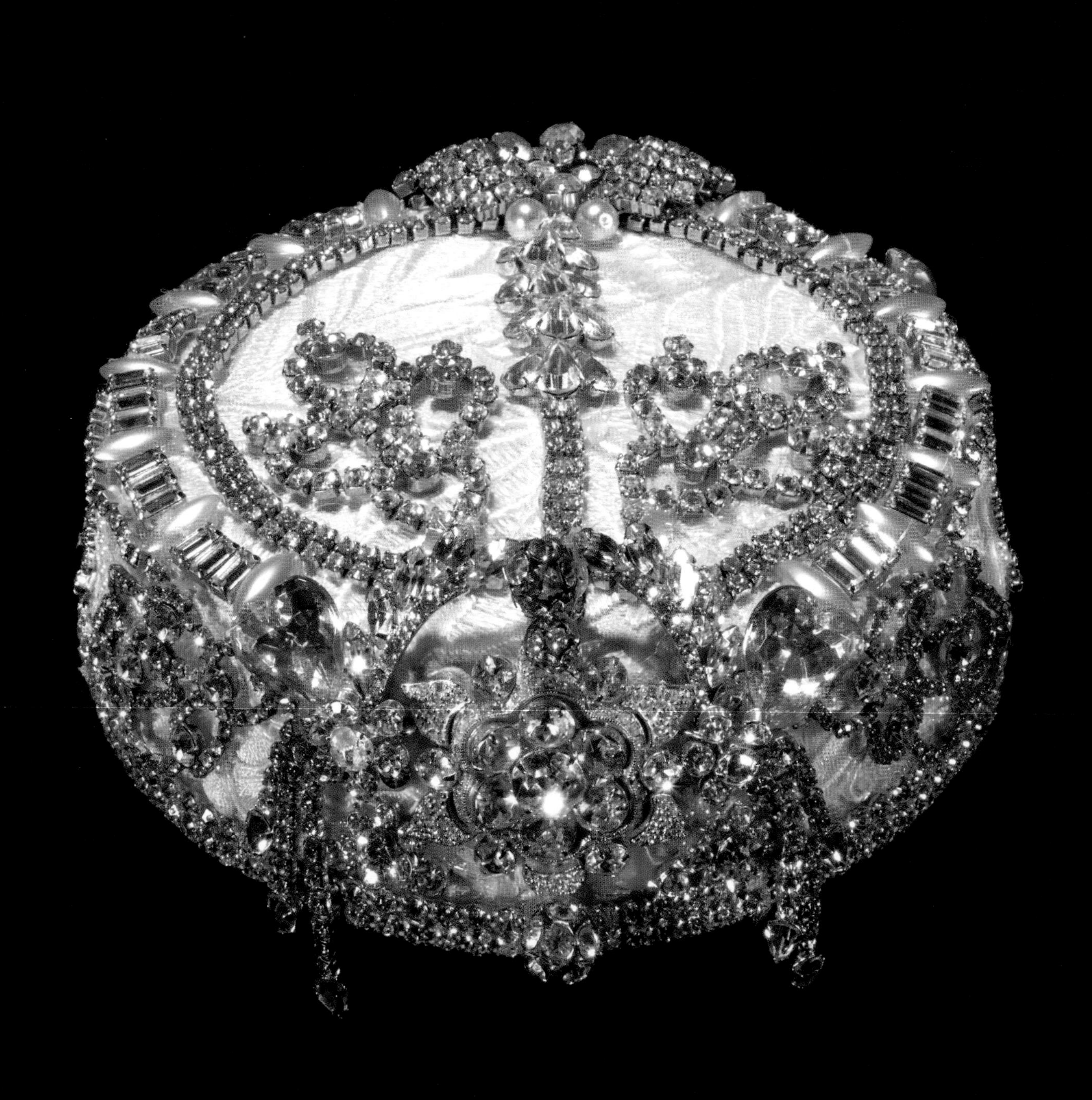

PLATE 189

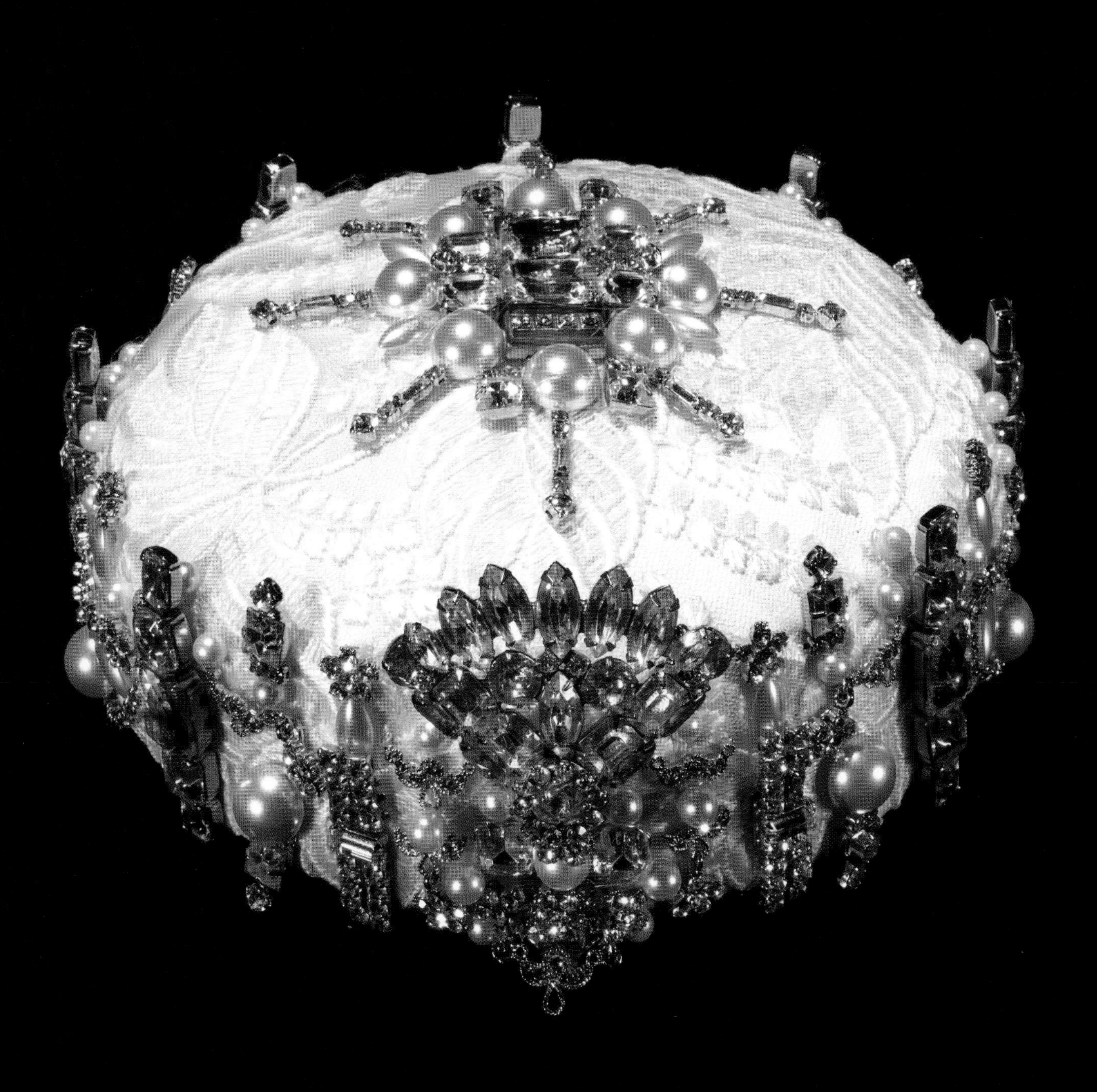

Plate 190

Plate 191

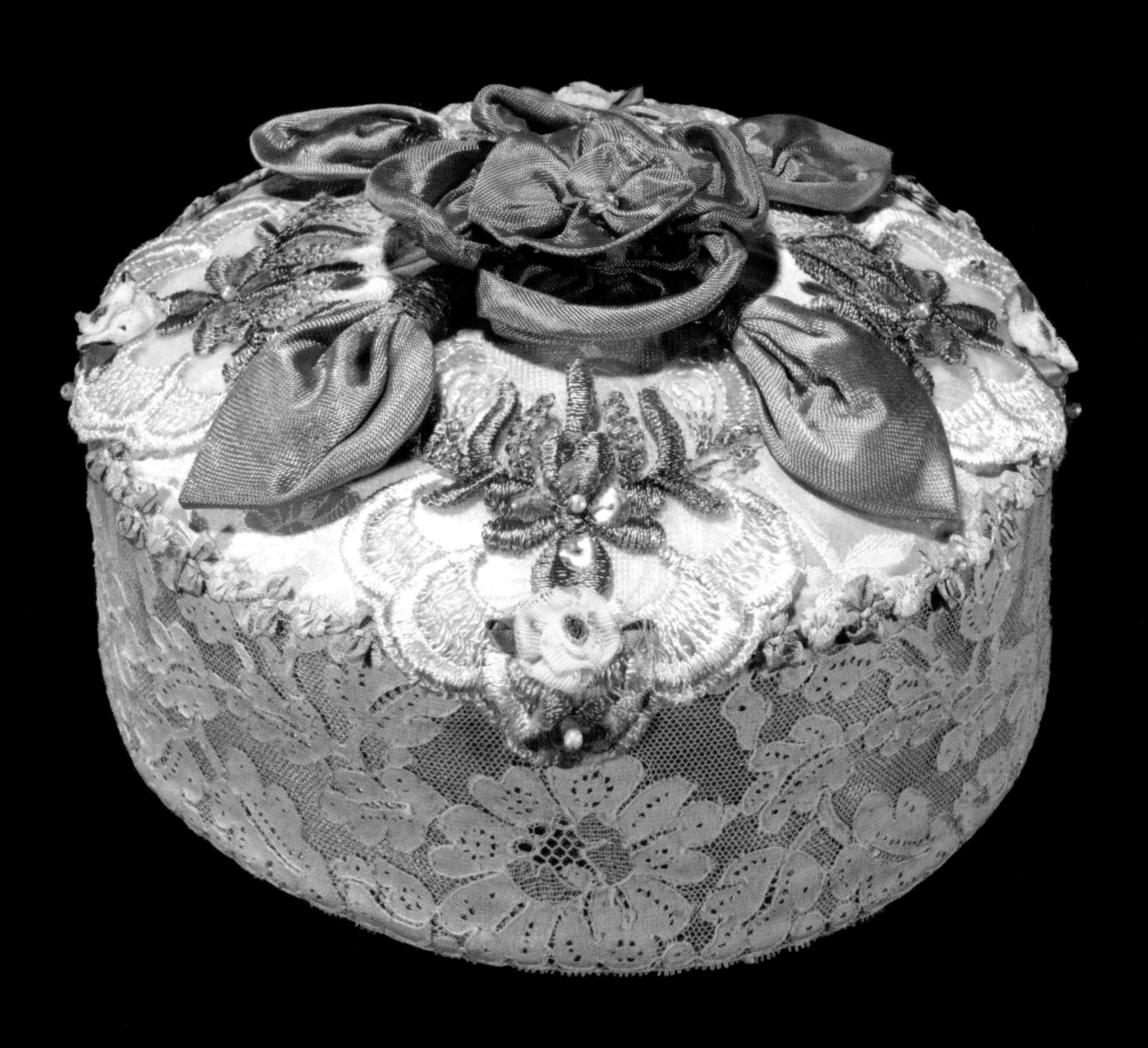

PLATE 192

PLATE 193

PLATE 194

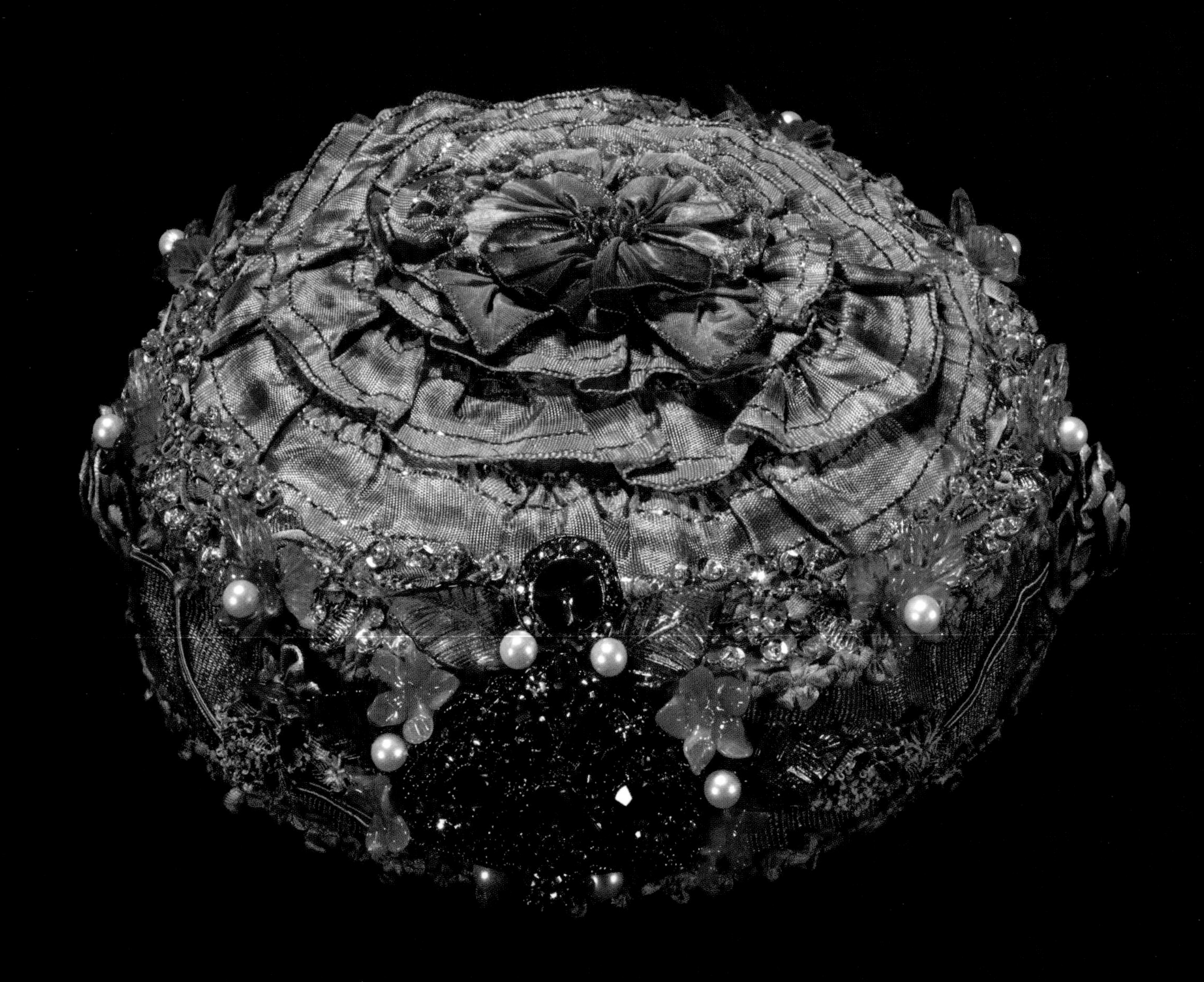

Plate 195

PLATE 196

Plate 197

PLATE 198

PLATE 199

Plate 200

PLATE 201

Plate 202

PLATE 203

Plate 204

Plate 205

Plate 206

Plate 207

Plate 208

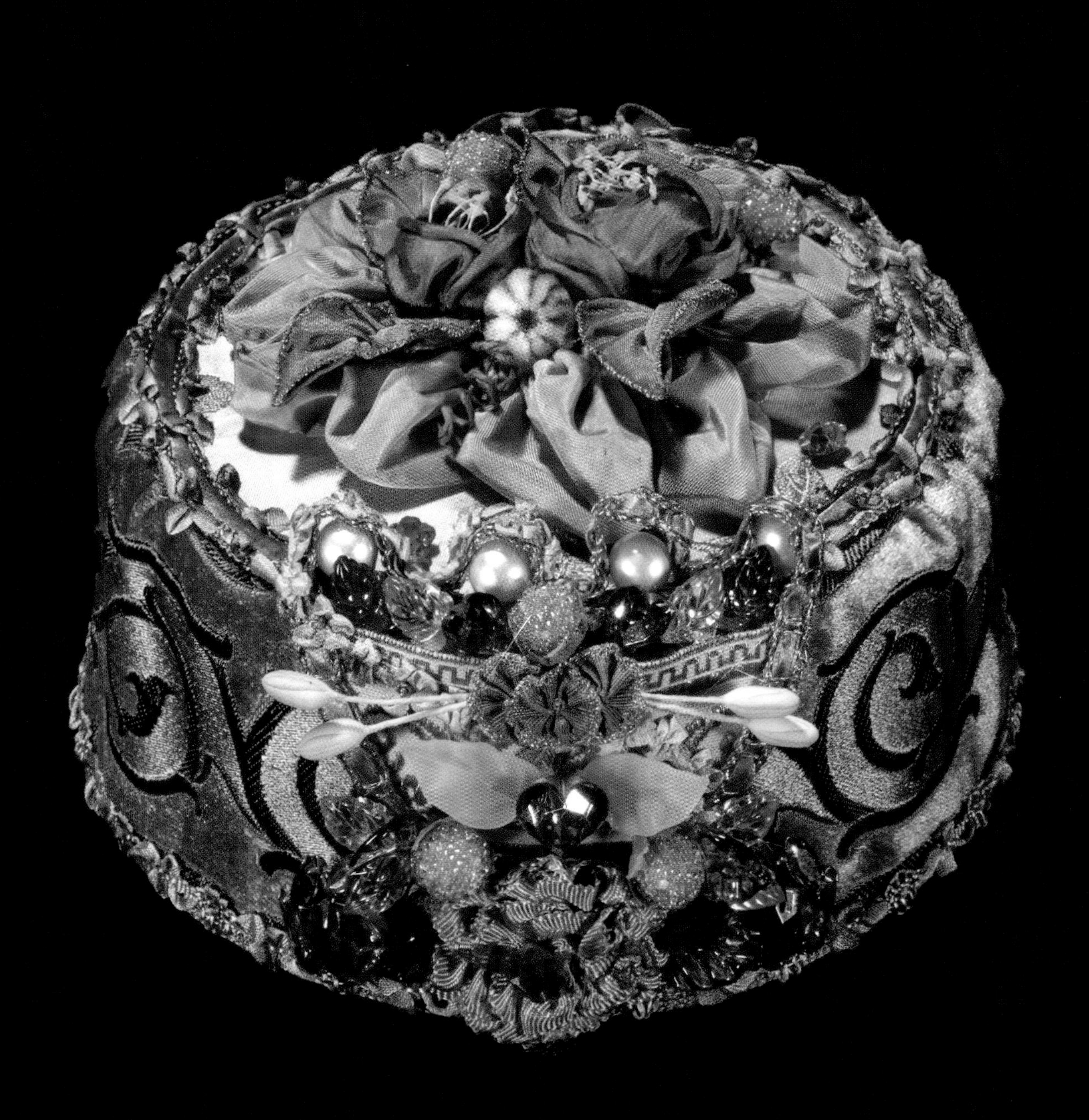

Plate 209

PLATE 210

Plate 211

Plate 212

Plate 213

PLATE 214

PLATE 215

Plate 216

PLATE 217

PLATE 218

Plate 219

Plate 220

PLATE 221

PLATE 222

PLATE 223

Plate 224

Plate 225

PLATE 226

Plate 227

Plate 228

PLATE 229

PLATE 230

PLATE 231

PLATE 232

Plate 233

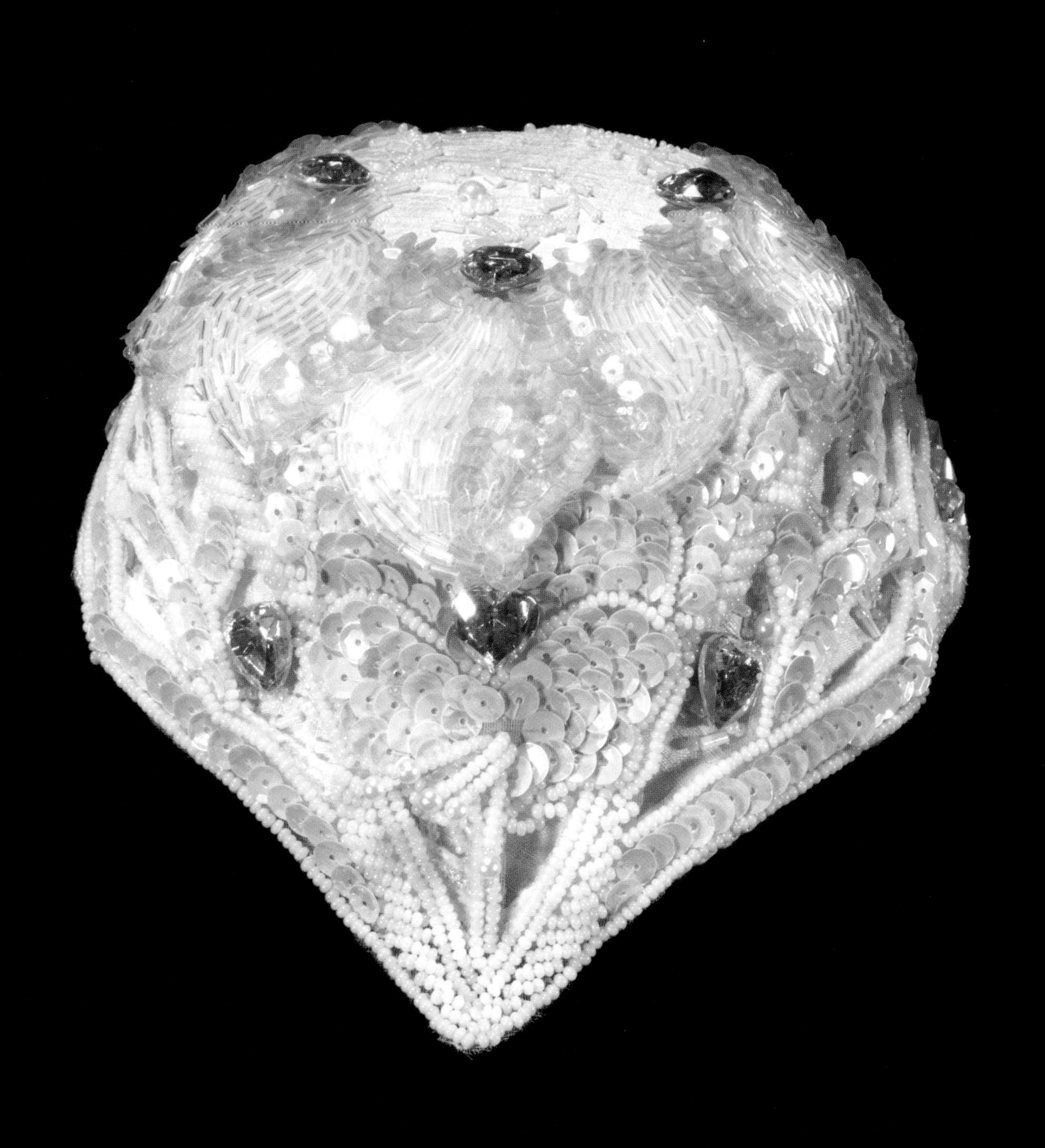

Plate 234

PLATE 235

Plate 236

Plate 237

PLATE 238

Plate 239

Plate 240

PLATE 241

PLATE 242

PLATE 243

PLATE 244

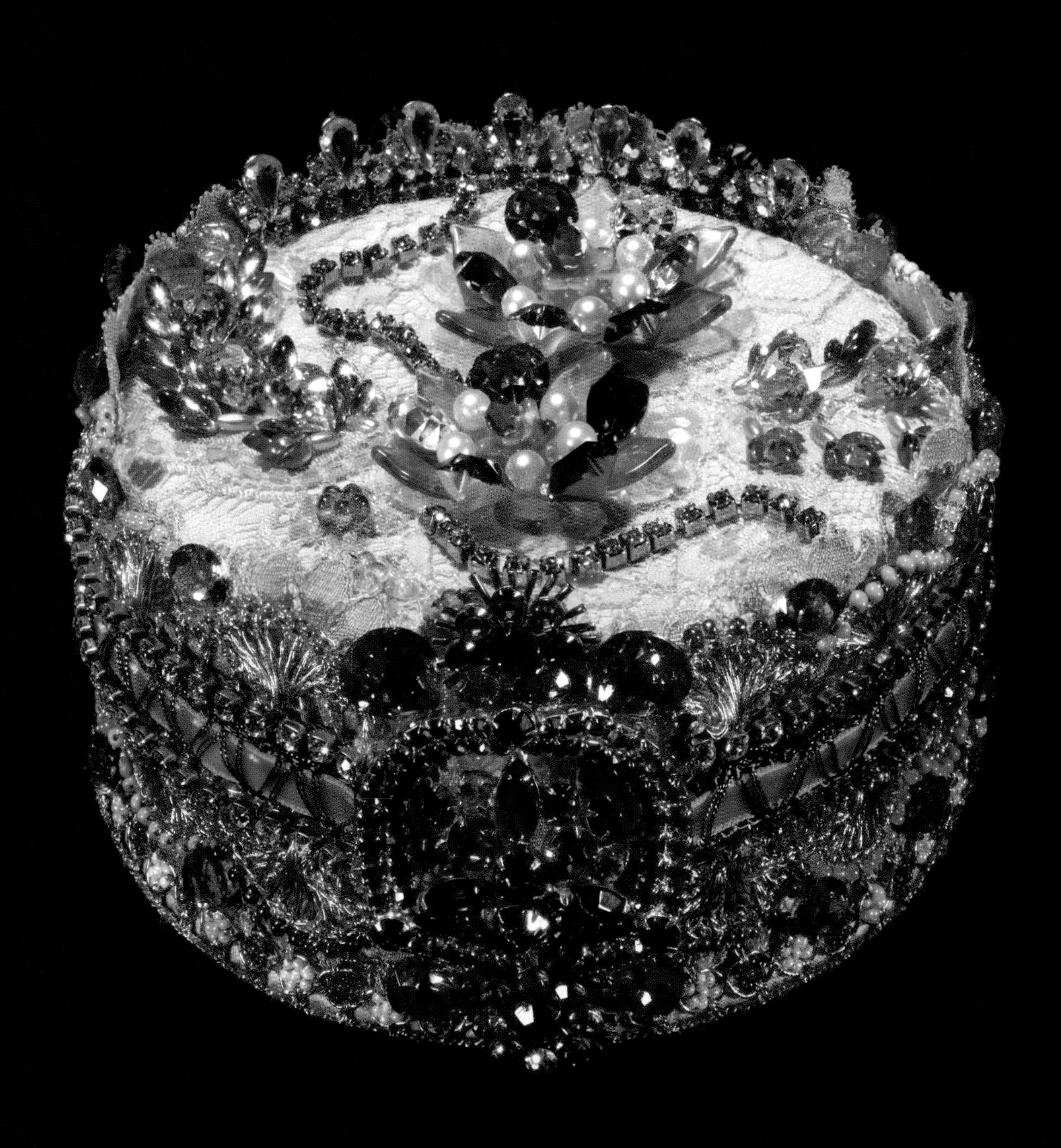

Plate 245

PLATE 250

PLATE 251

PLATE 252

Plate 253

PLATE 254

Plate 255

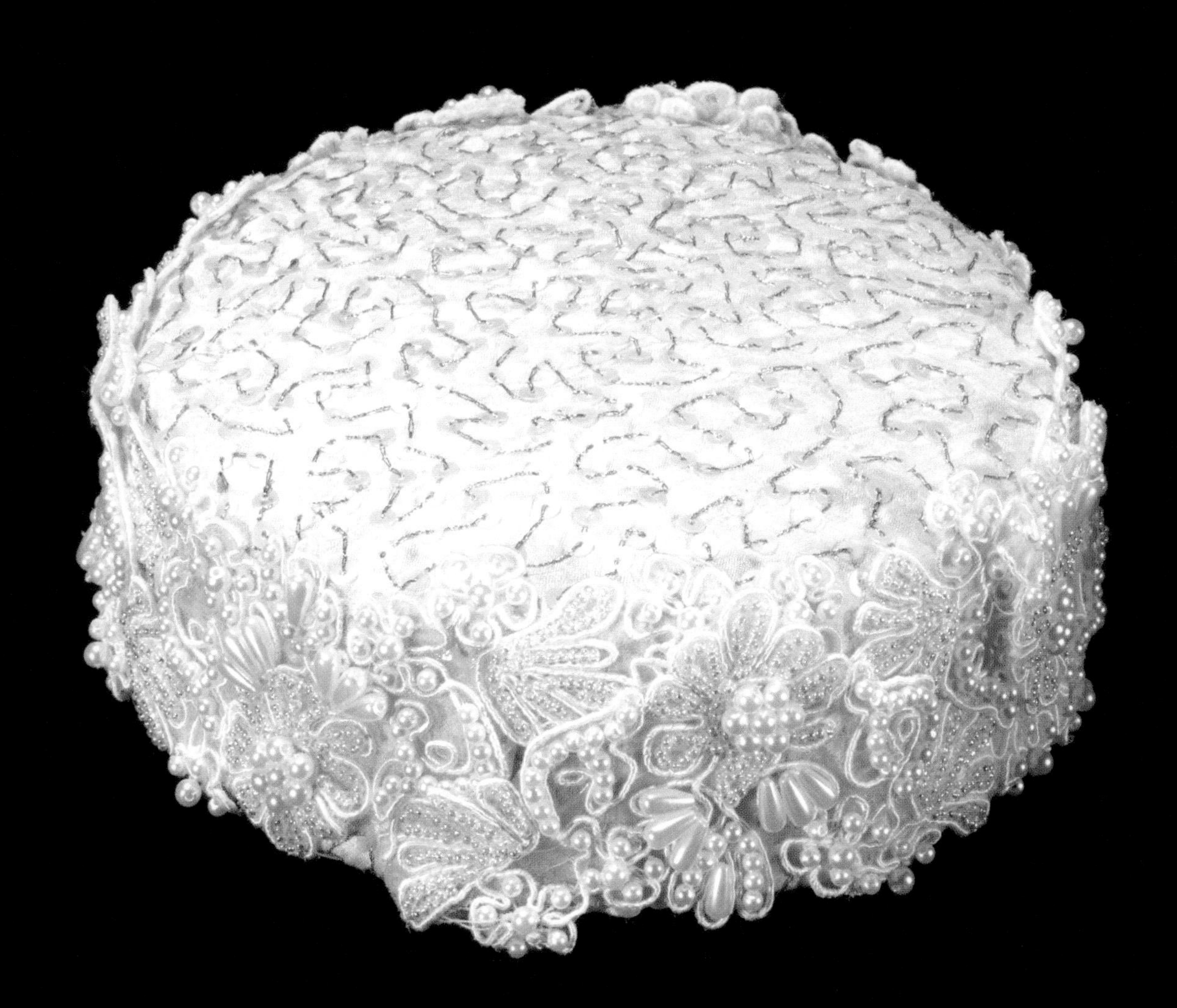

Plate 256

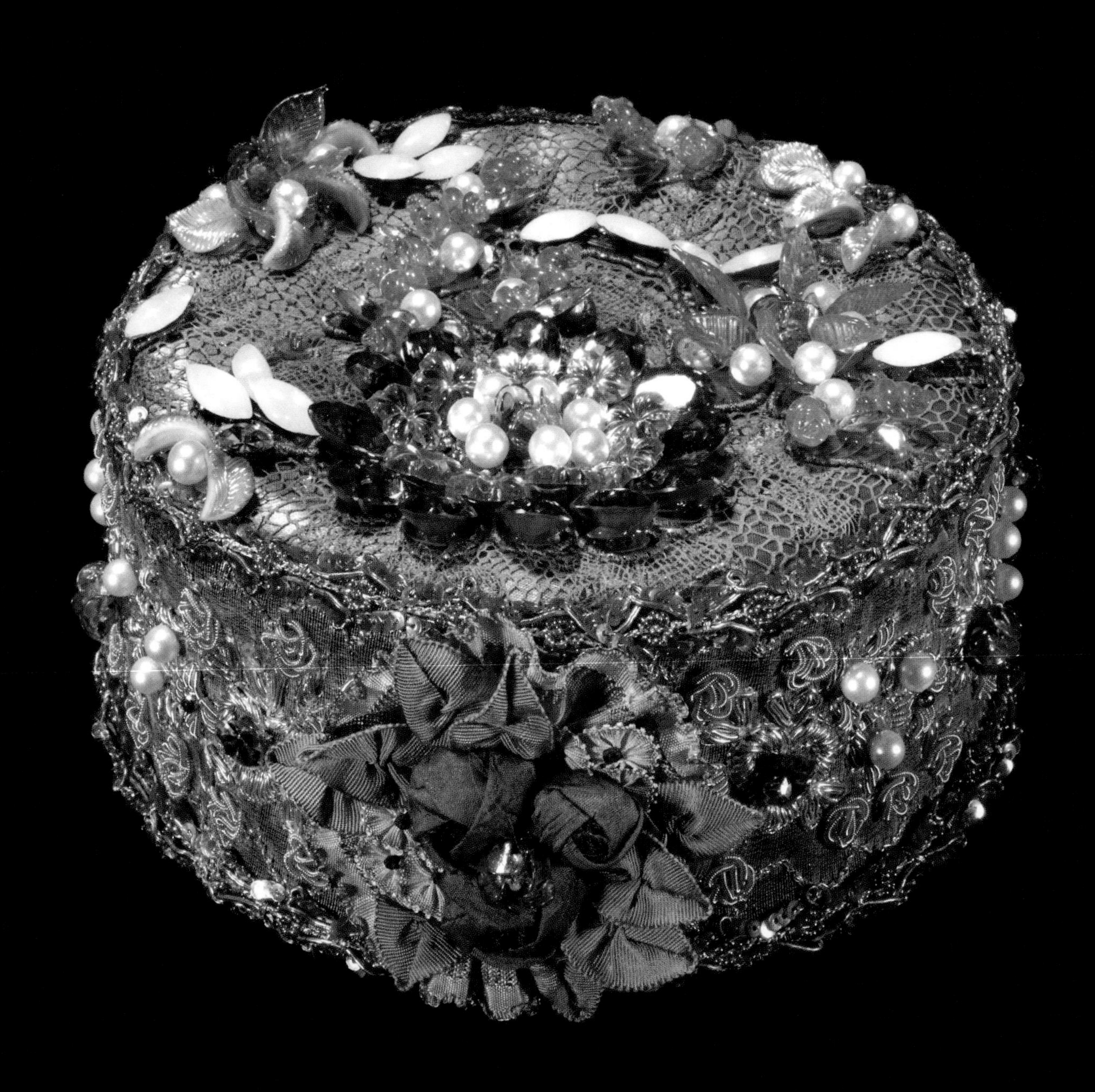

PLATE 257

Plate 258

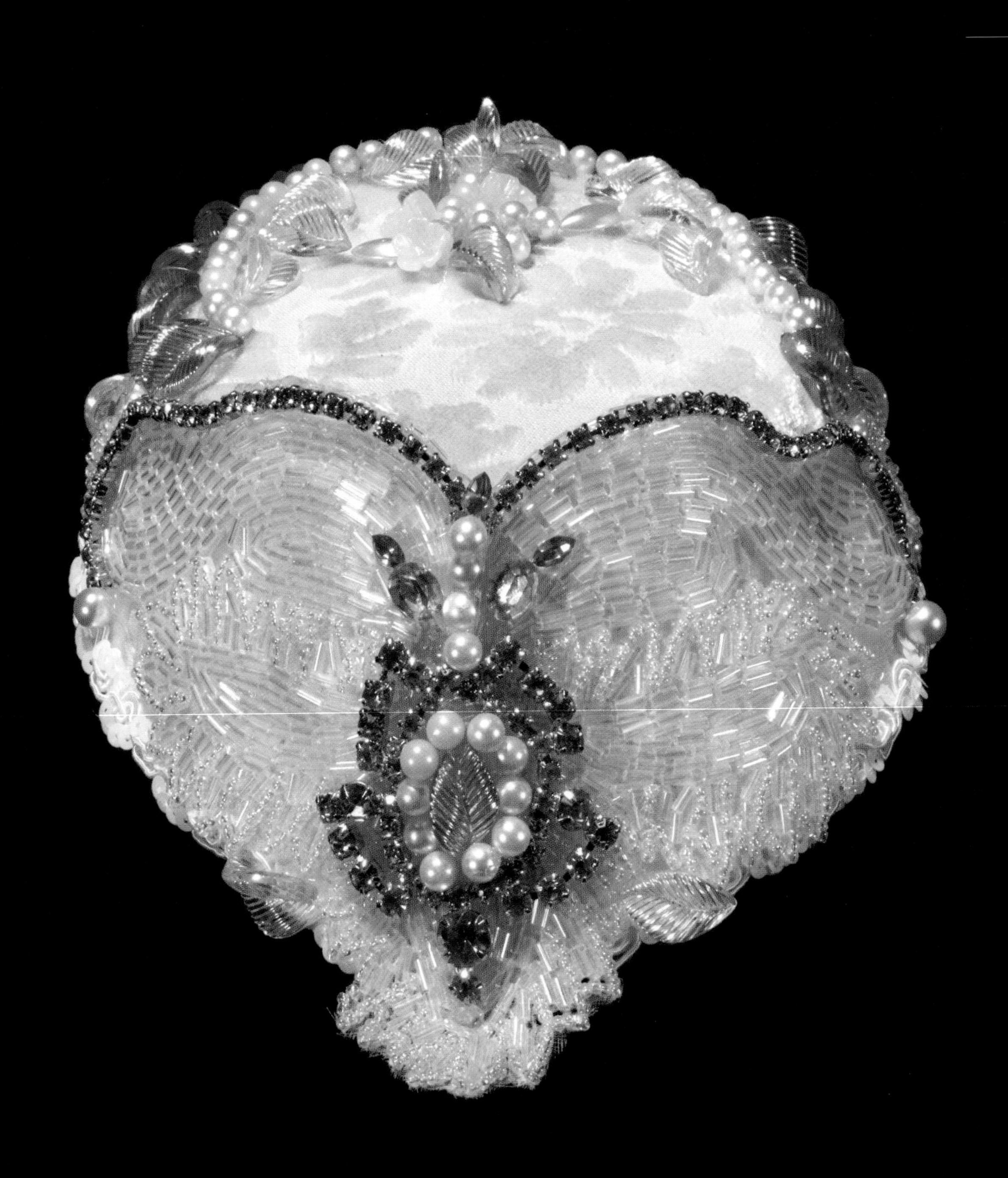

PLATE 259

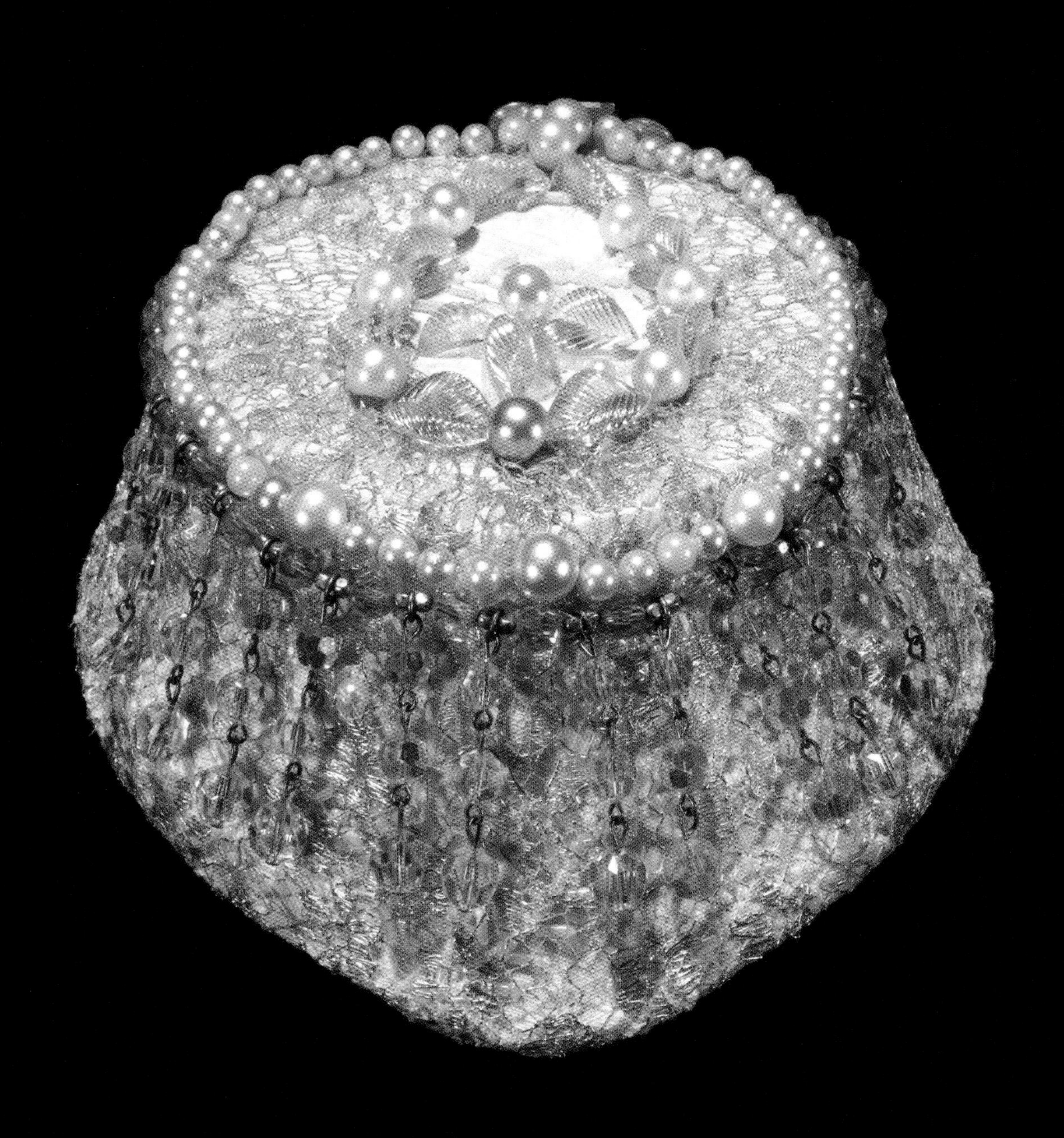

Plate 260

Plate 261

Plate 262

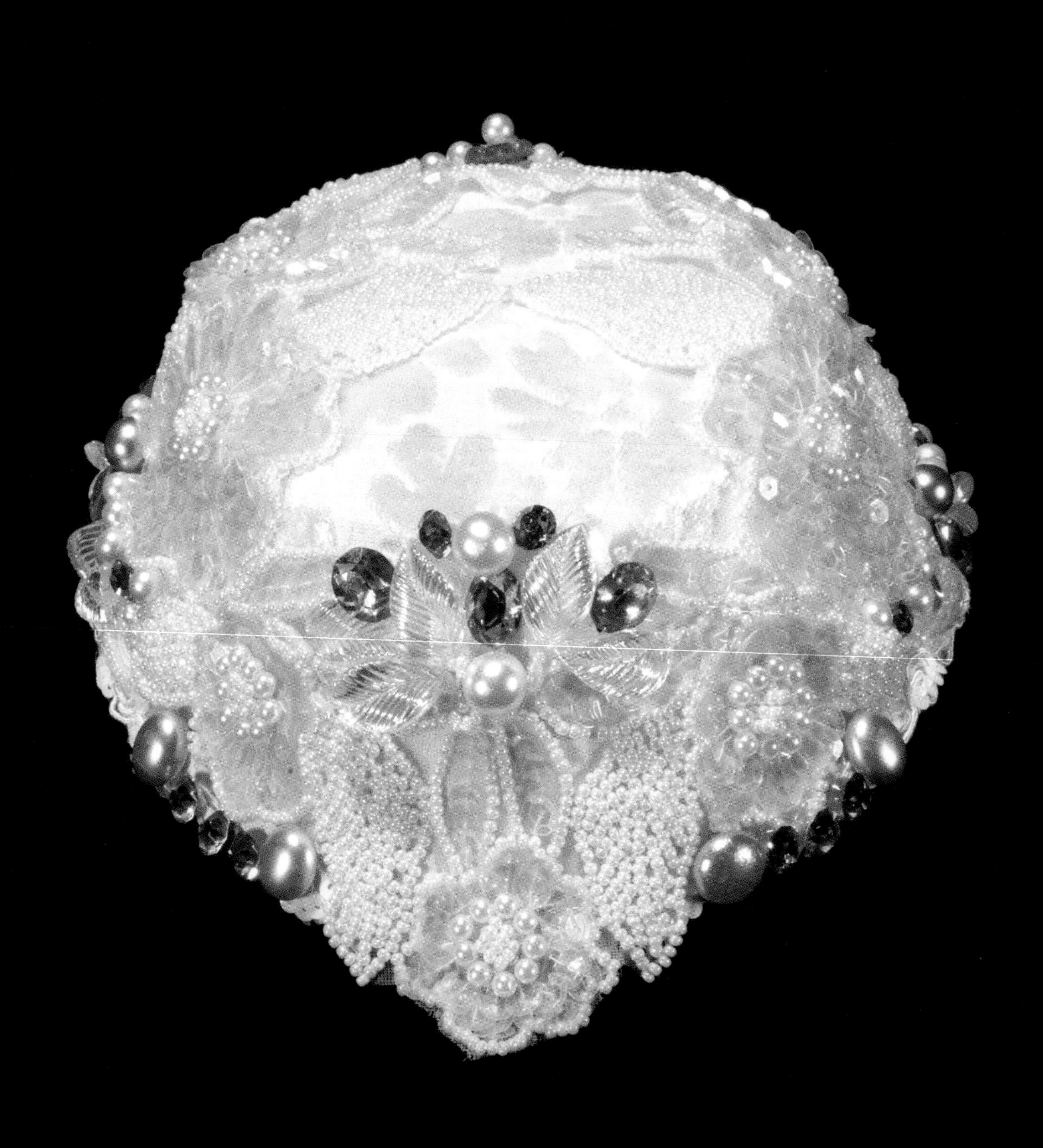

PLATE 263

PLATE 264

PLATE 265

PLATE 266

Headbands

Plate 267

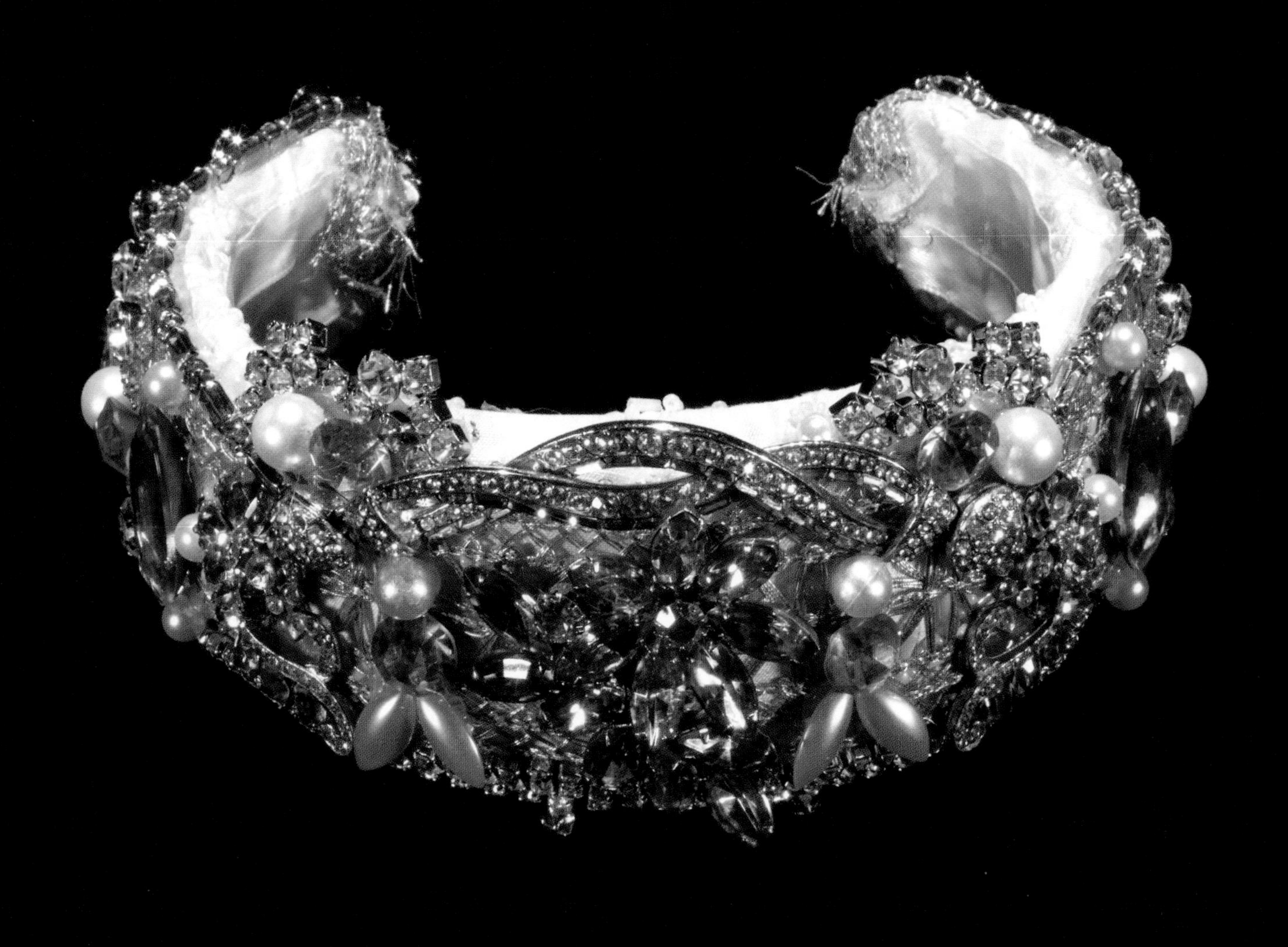

Plate 268

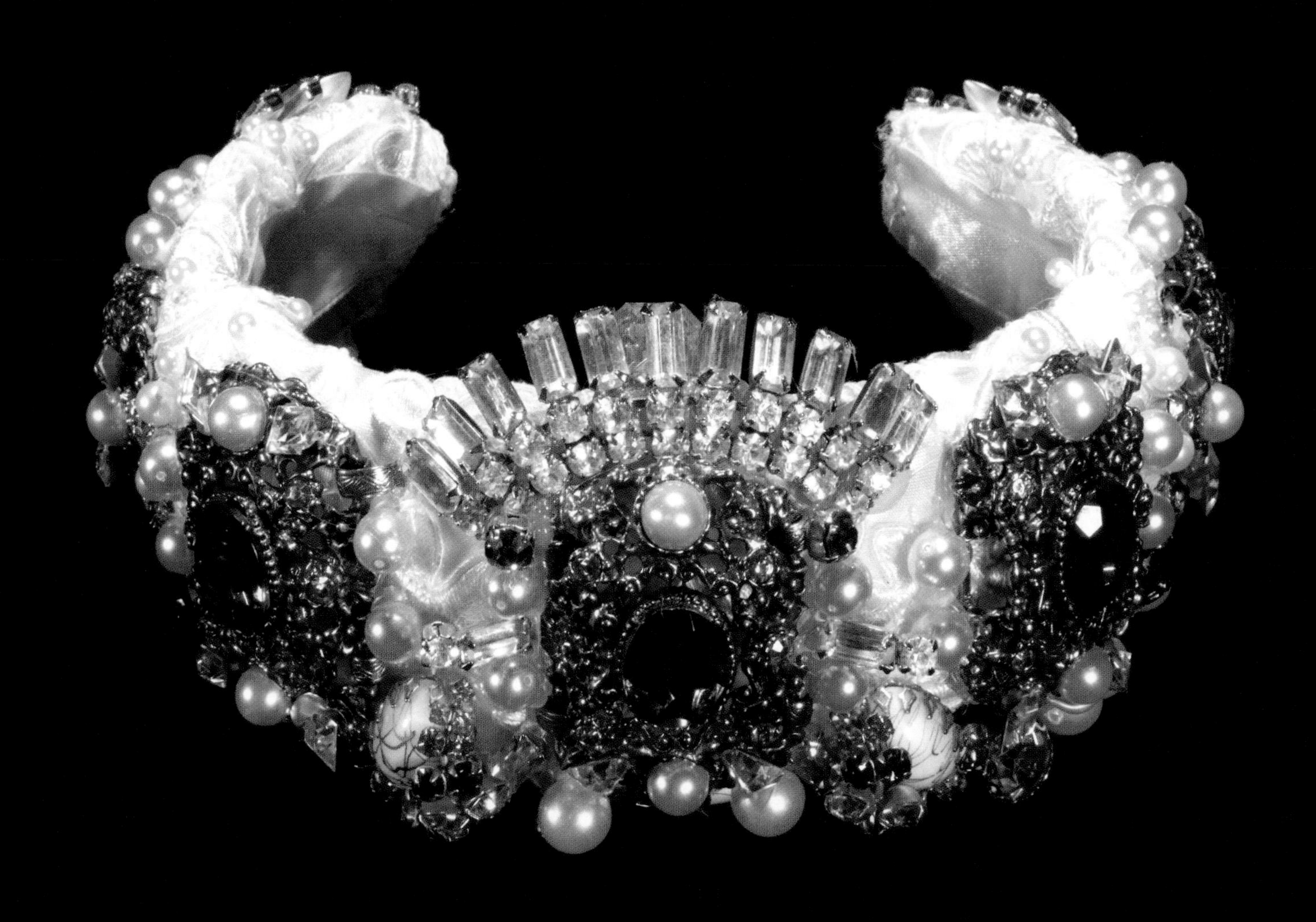

PLATE 269

PLATE 270

PLATE 271

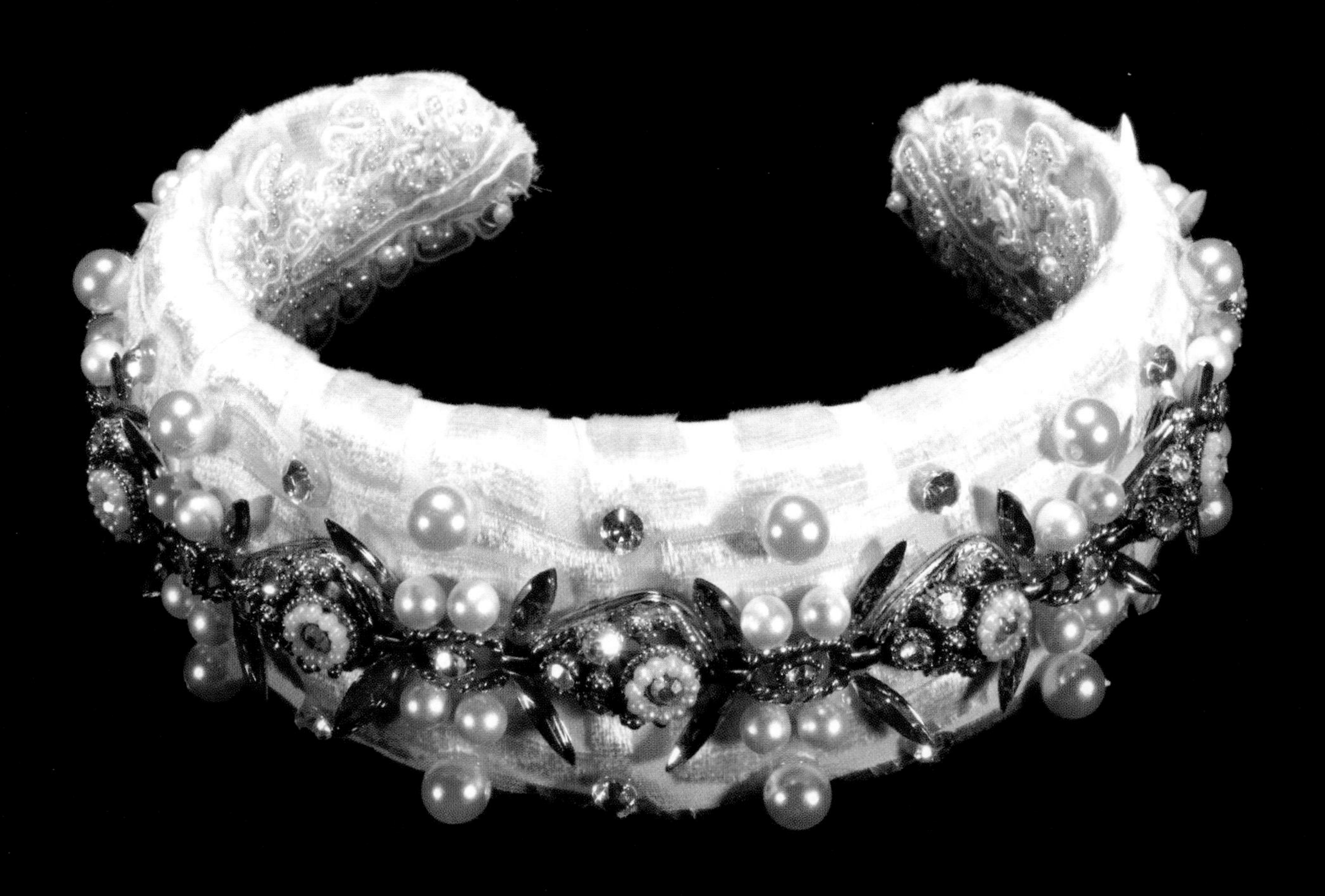

Plate 272

PLATE 273

Plate 274

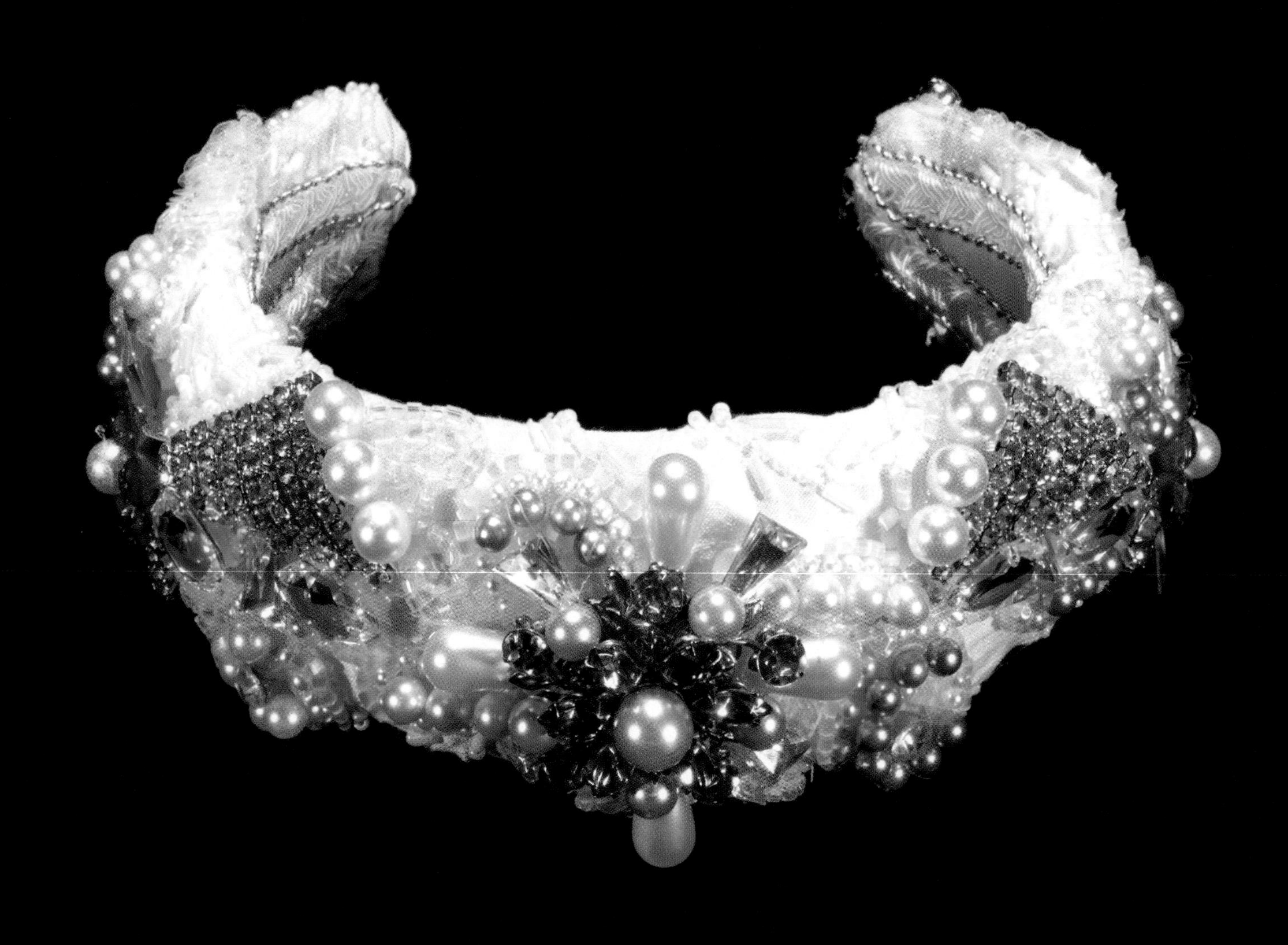

Plate 275

Plate 276

Plate 277

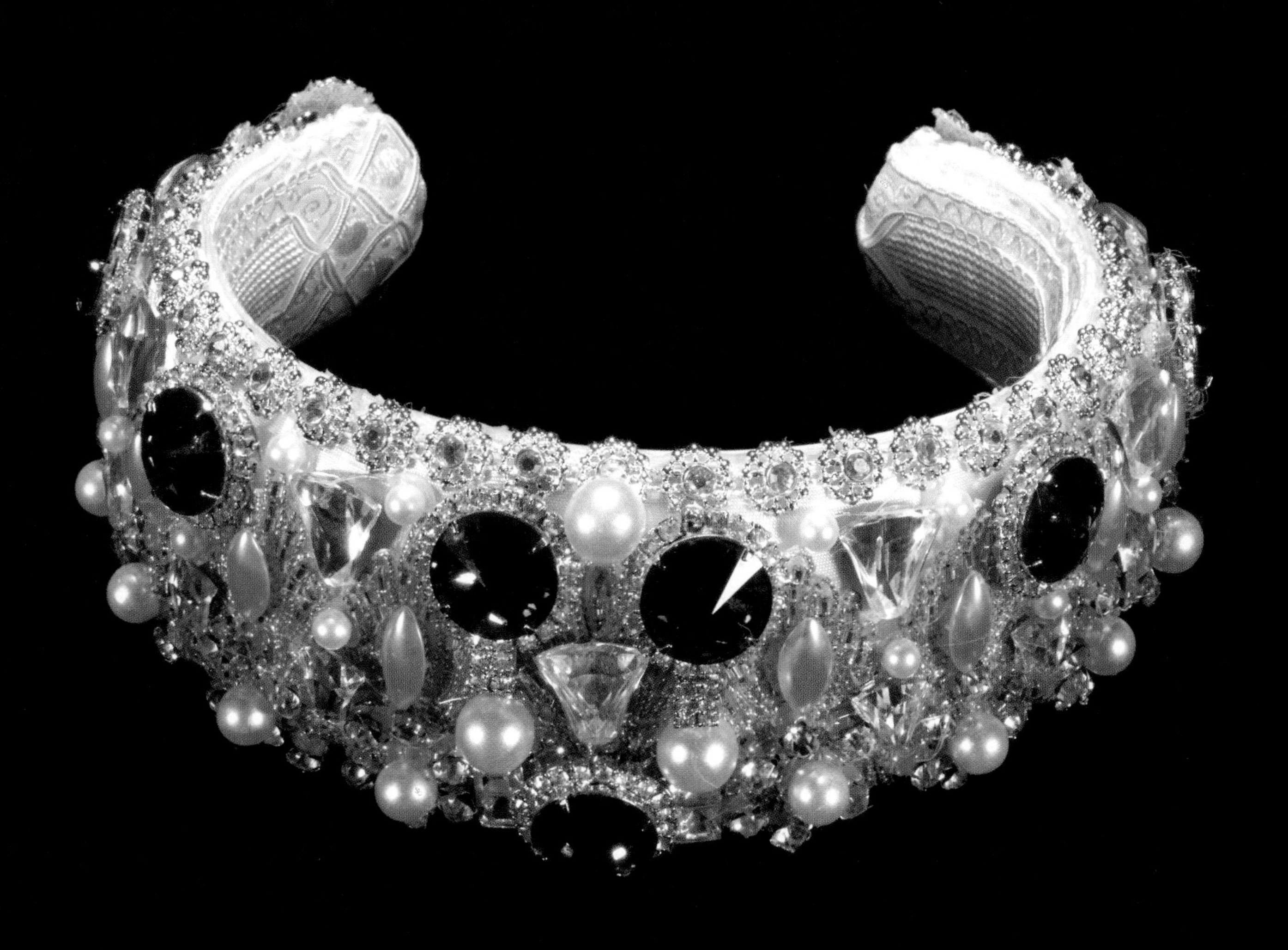

PLATE 278

PLATE 279

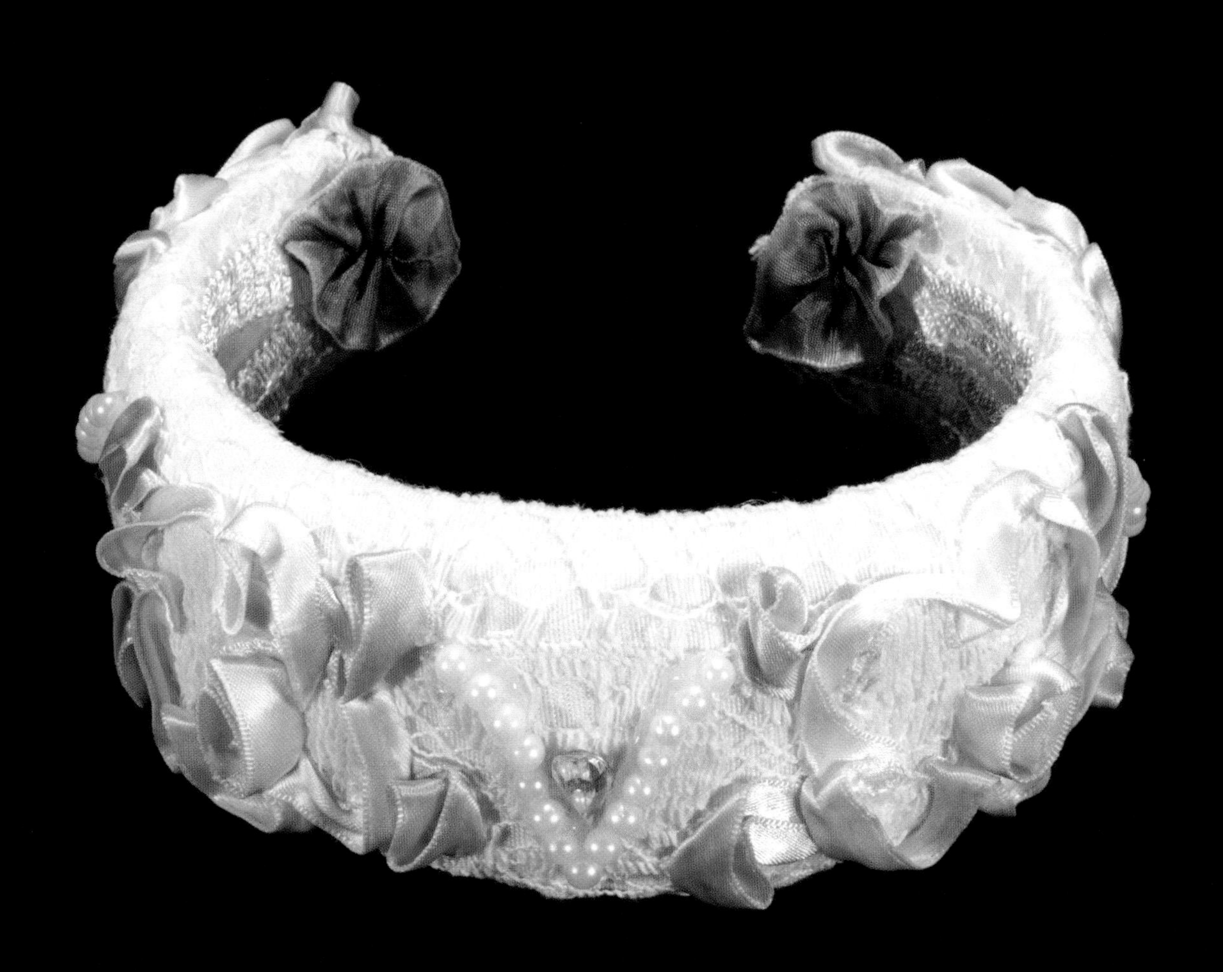

Plate 280

PLATE 281

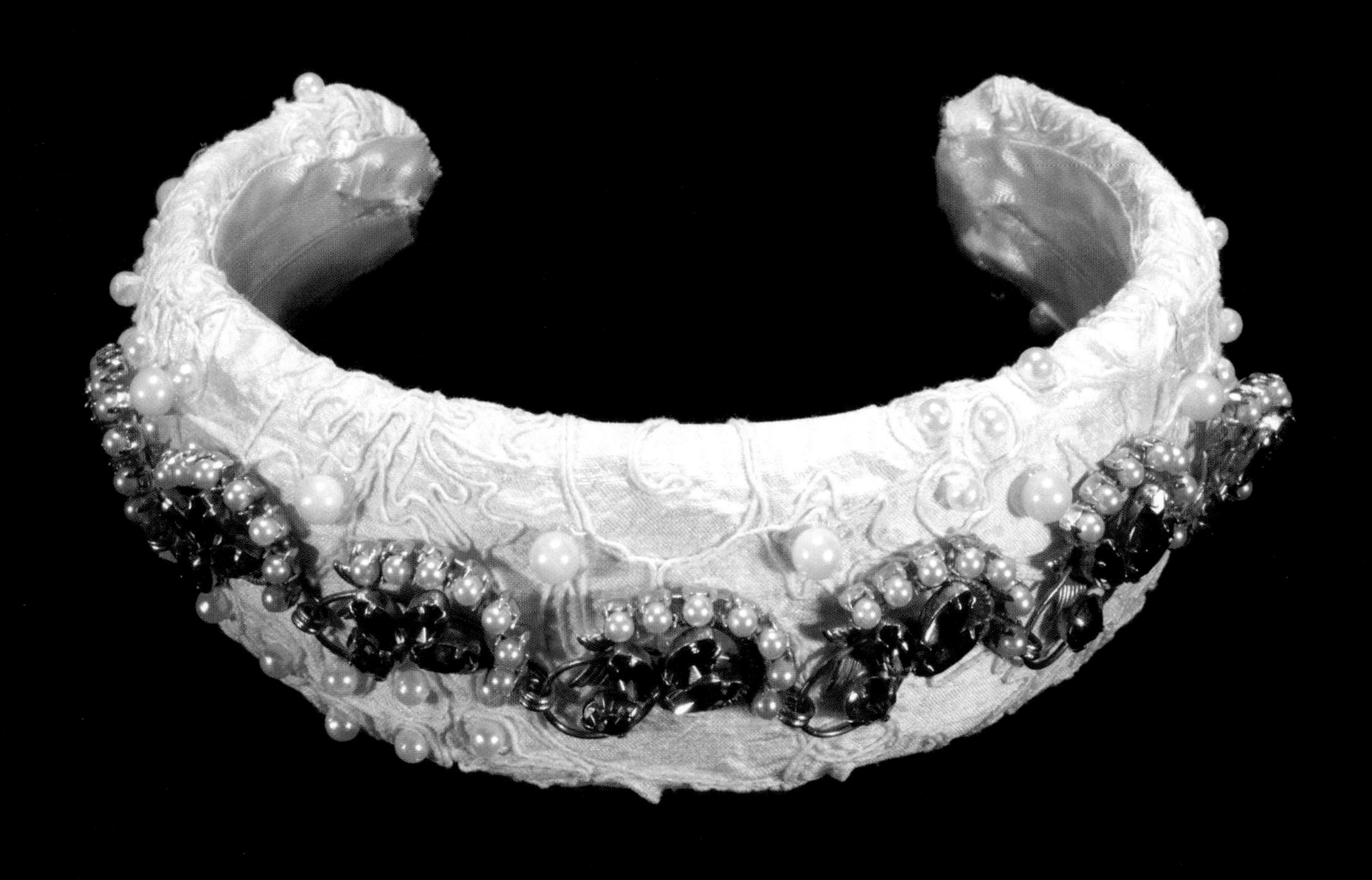

Plate 282

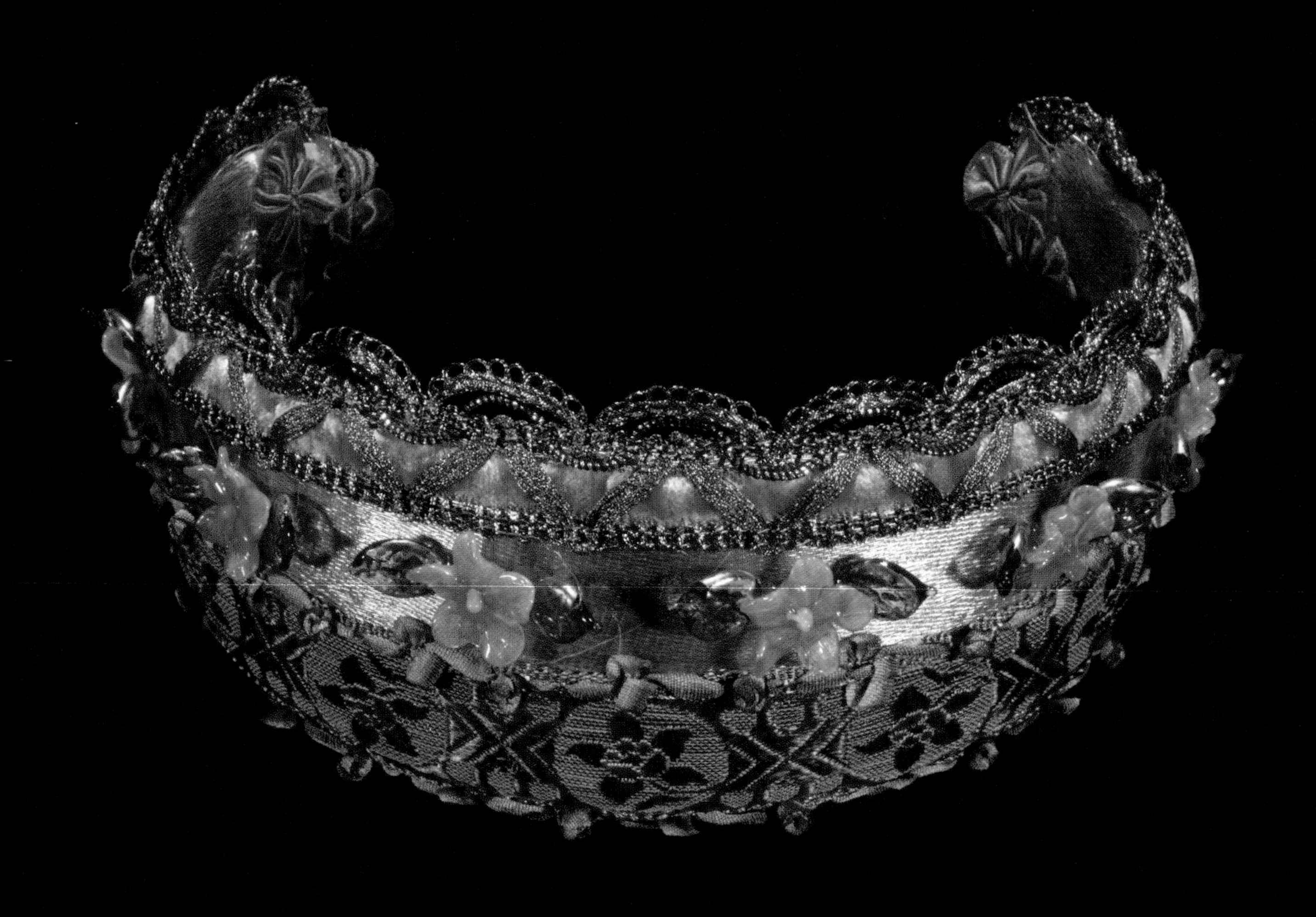

Plate 283

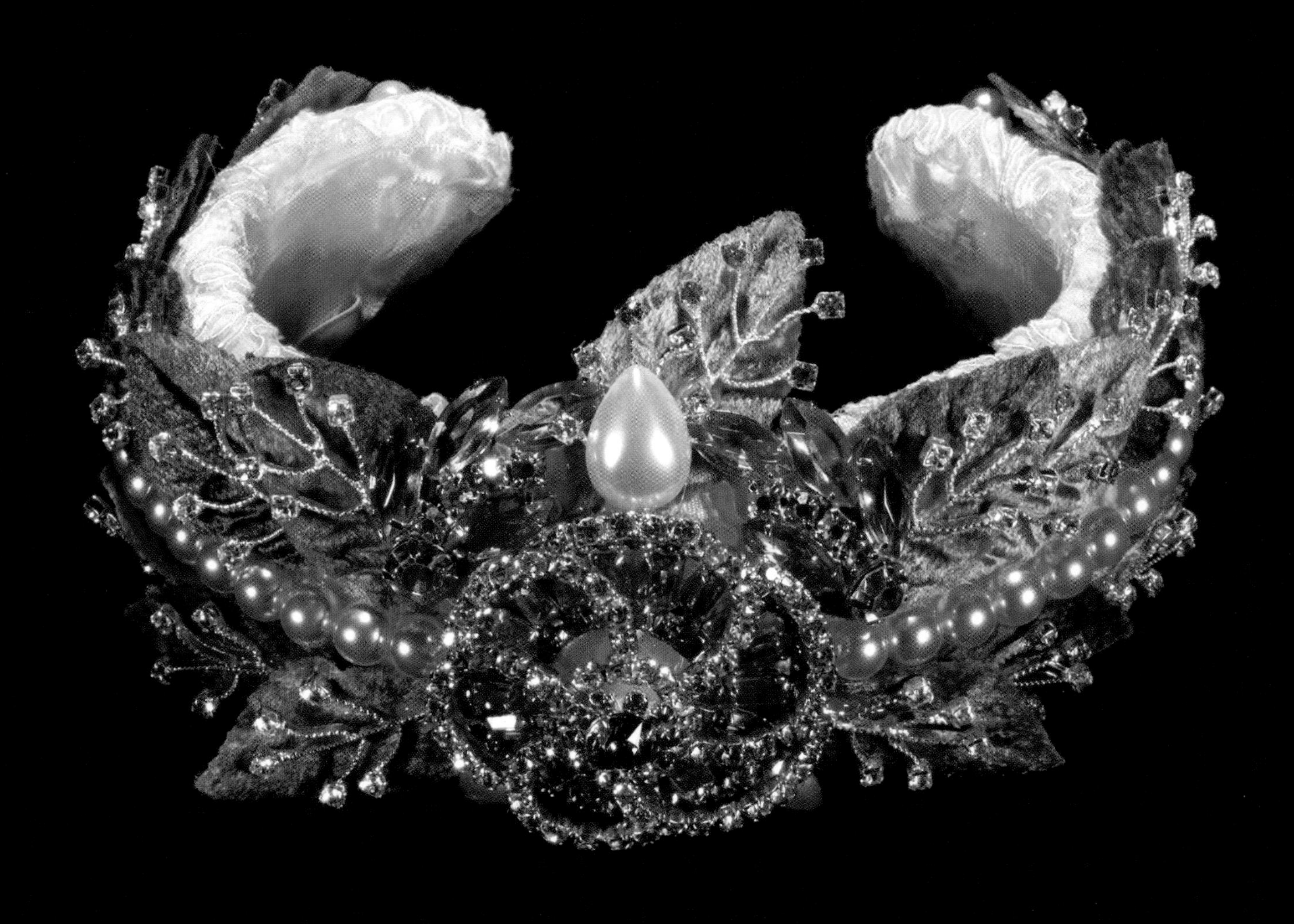

Plate 284

Plate 285

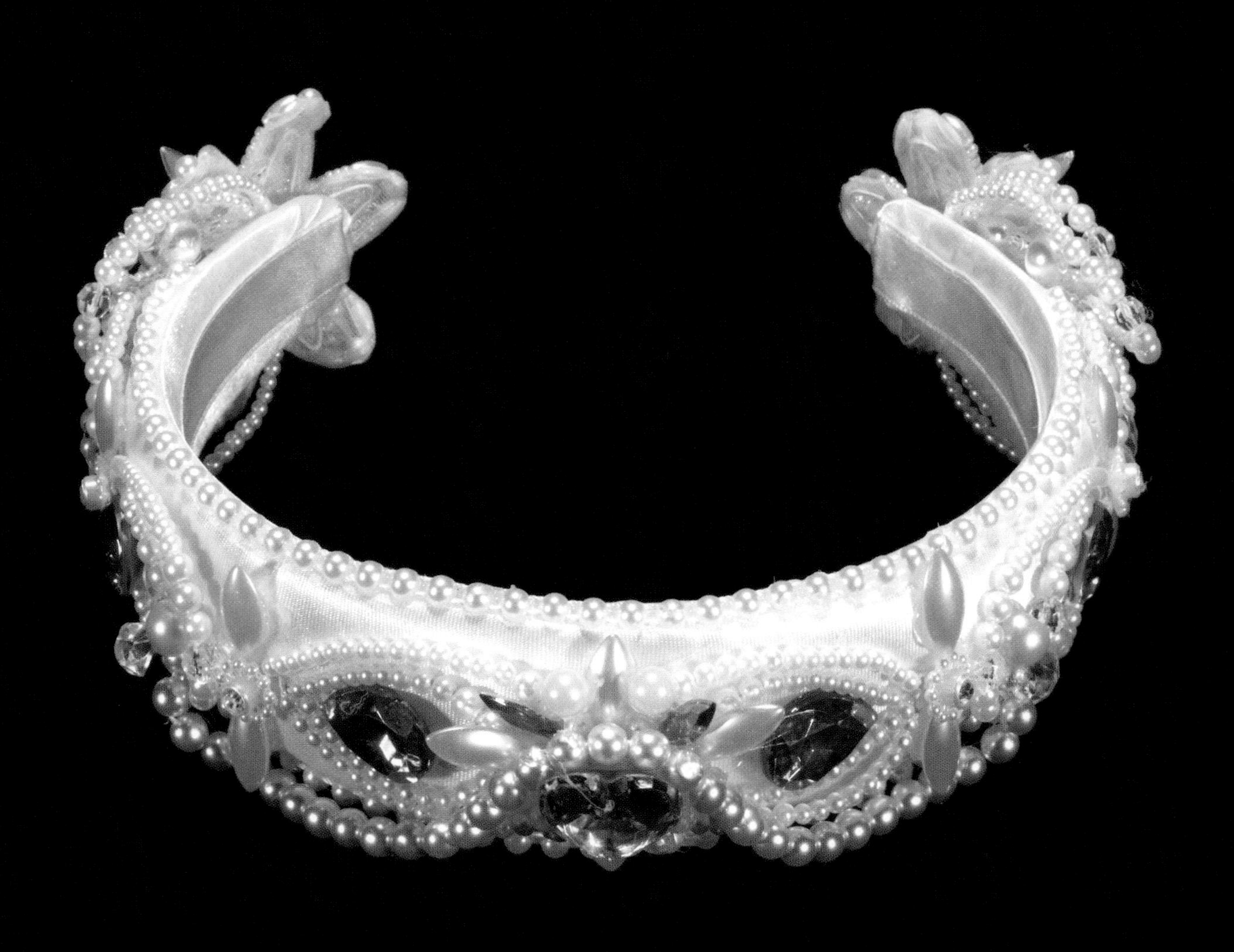

Plate 286

PLATE 287

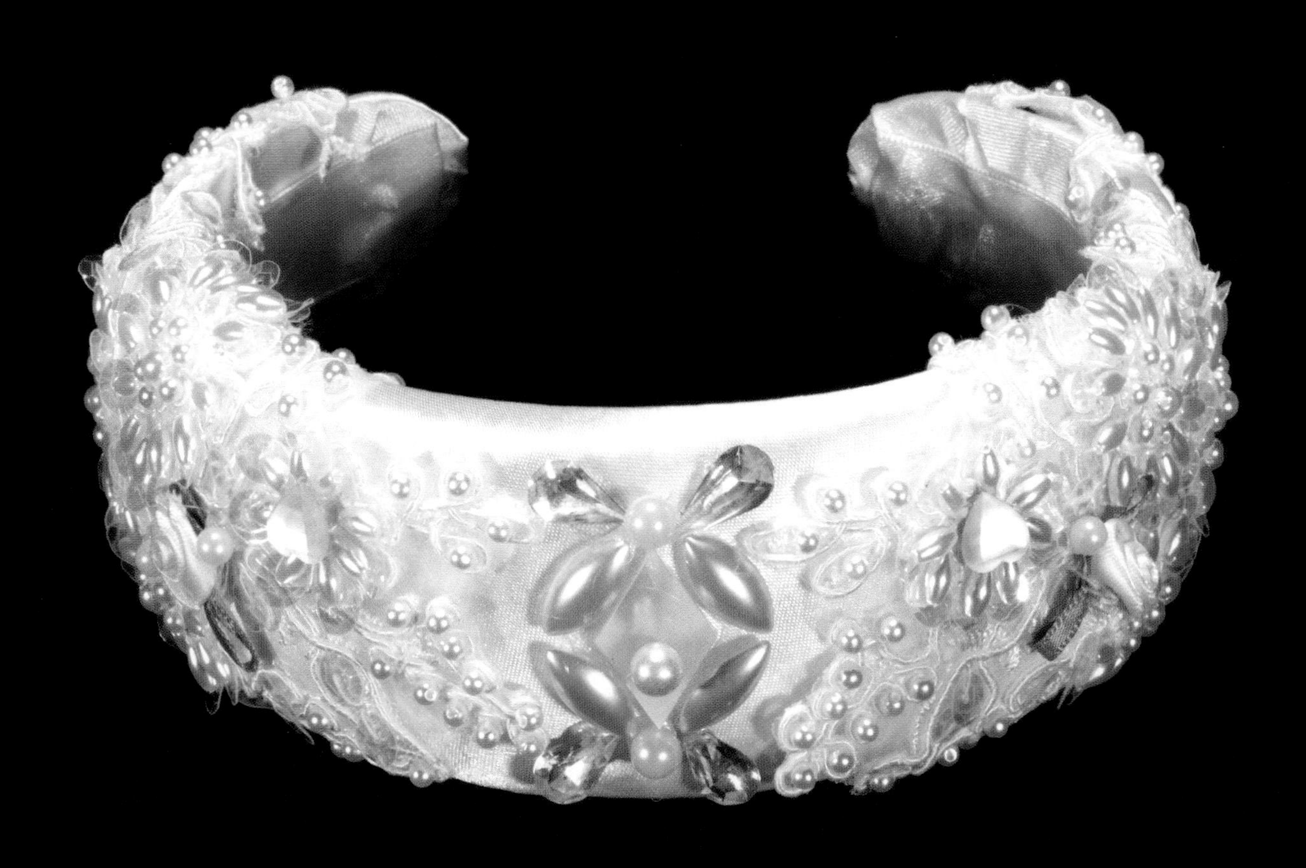

Plate 288

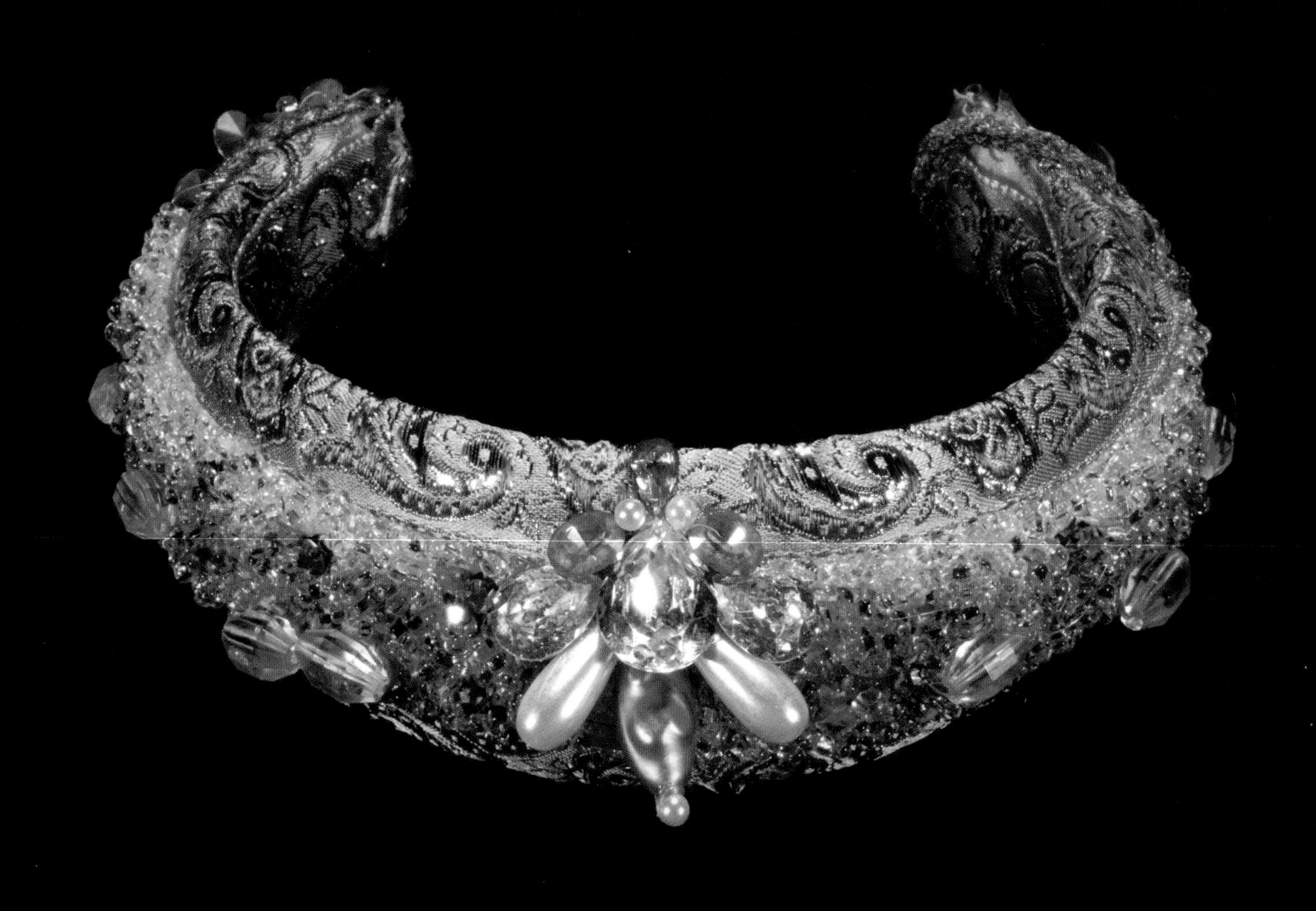

Plate 289

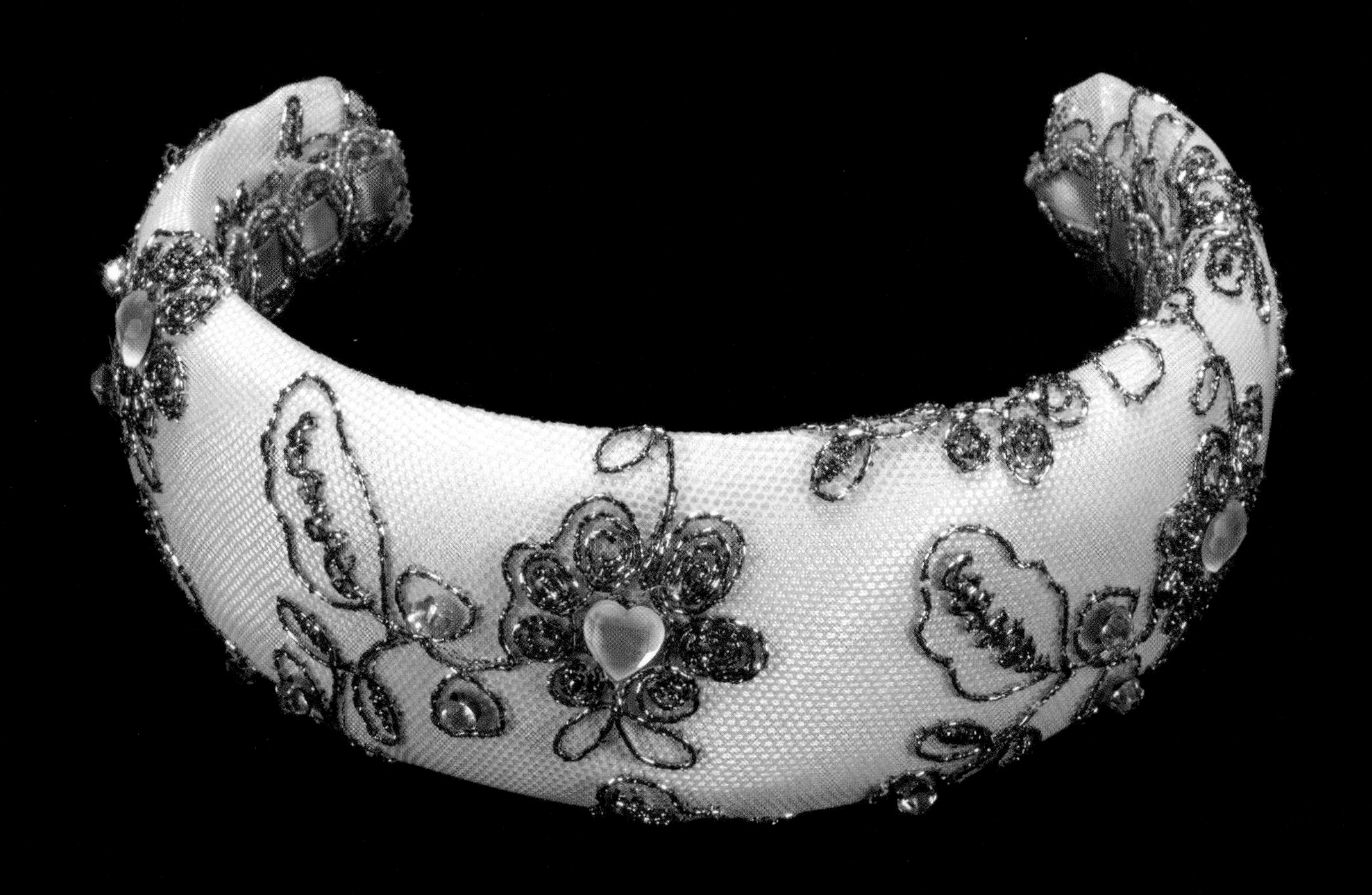

Plate 290

Plate 291

Plate 292

PLATE 293

Plate 294

Plate 295

Plate 296

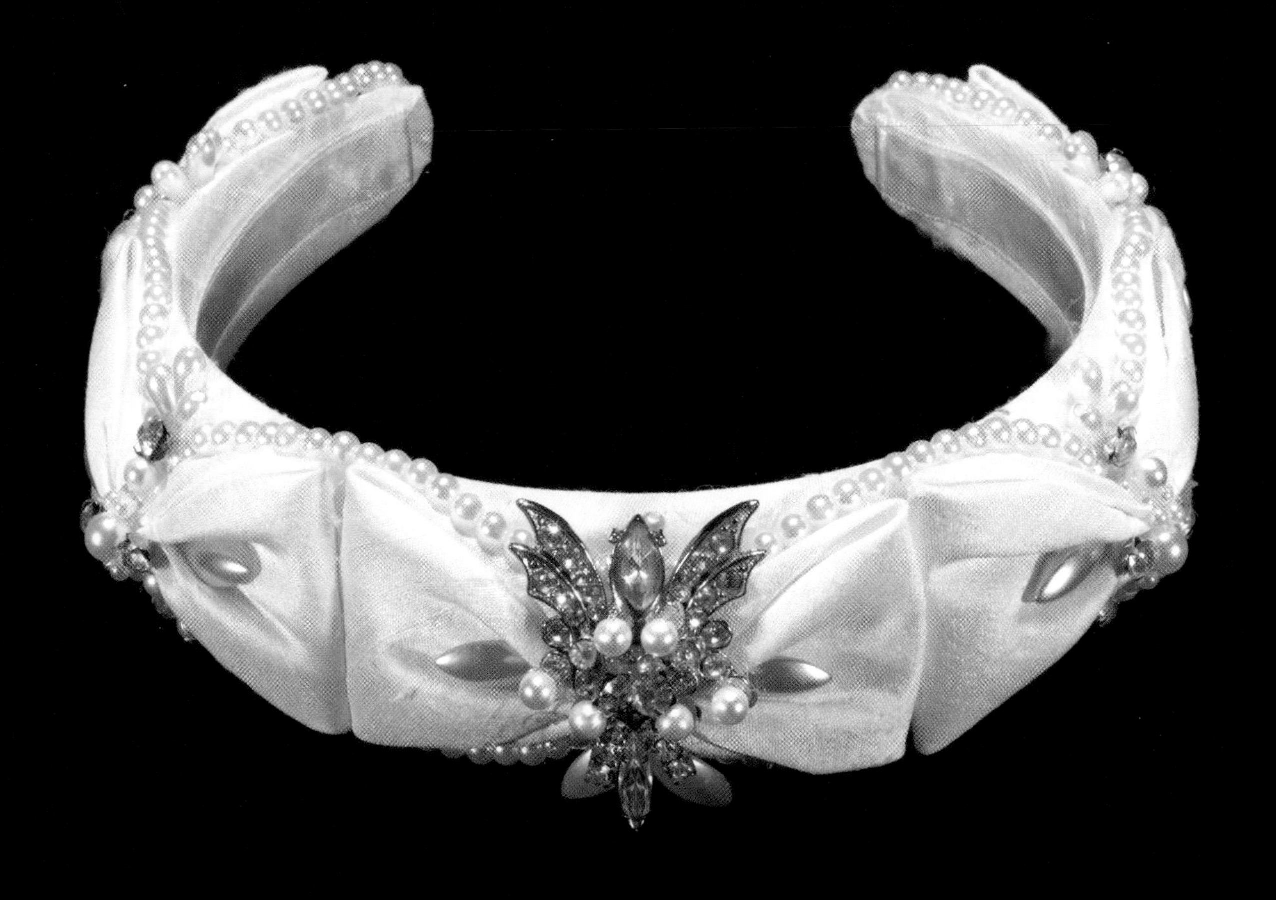

PLATE 297

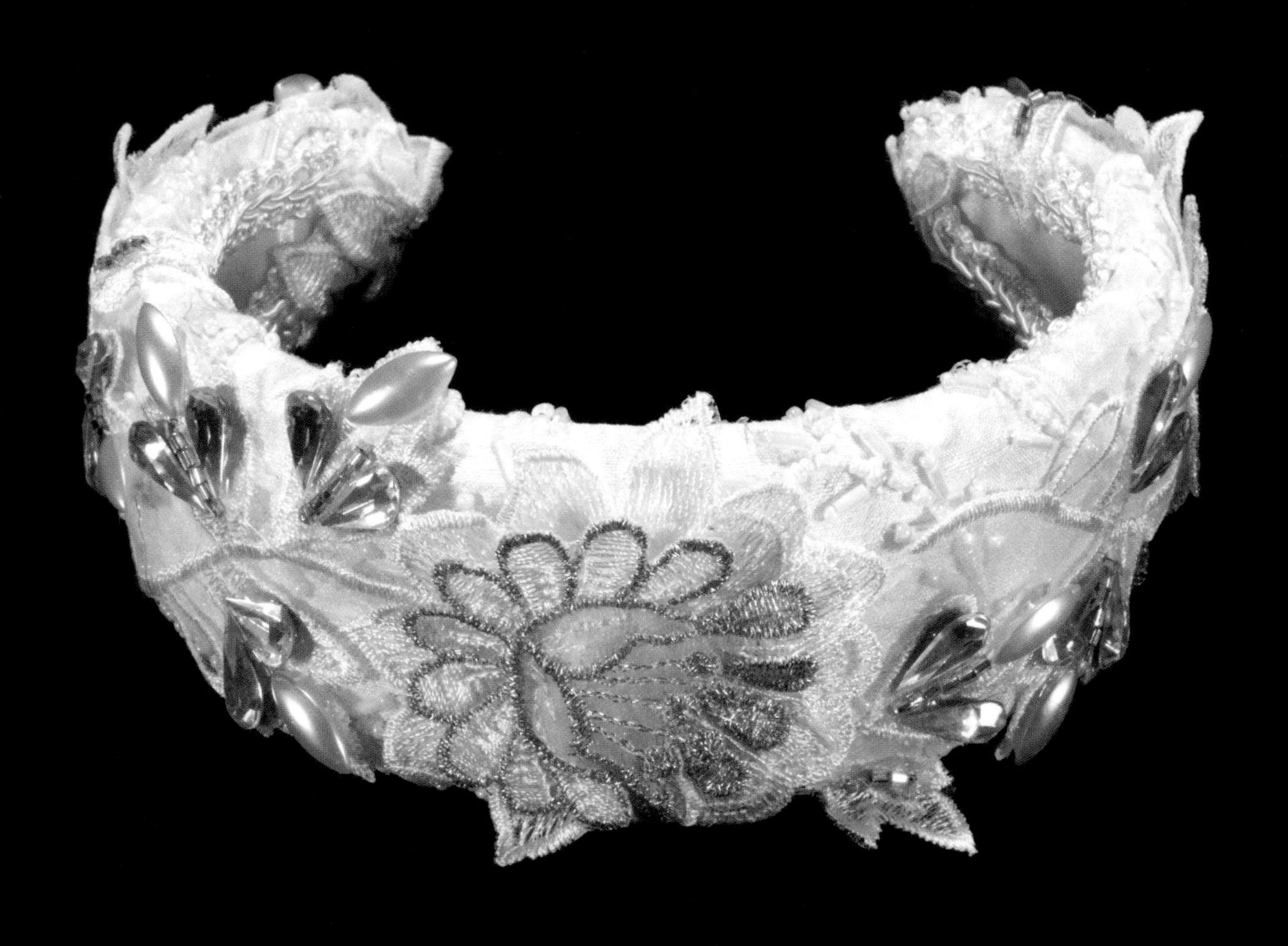

Plate 298

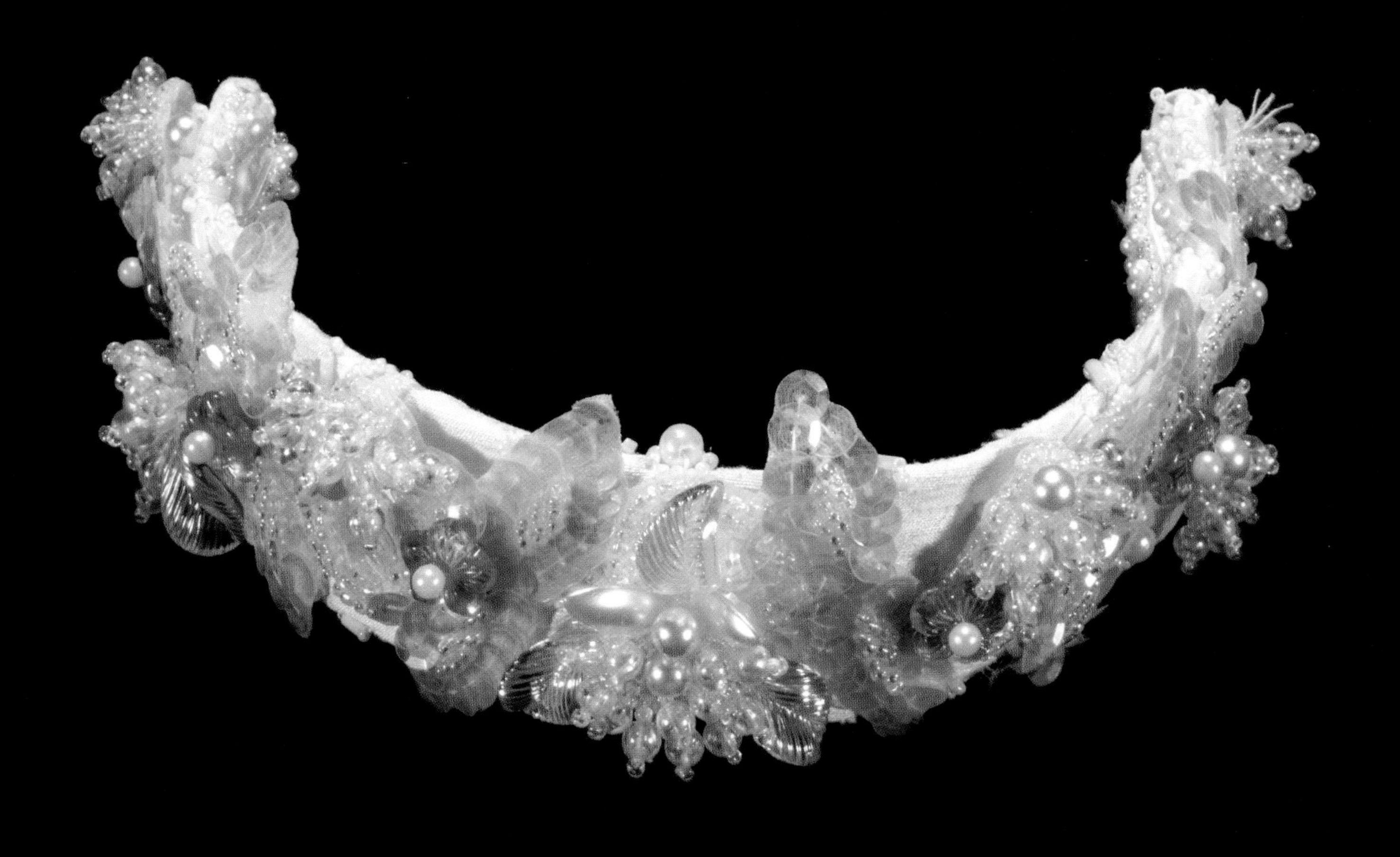

Plate 299

Plate 300

Plate 301

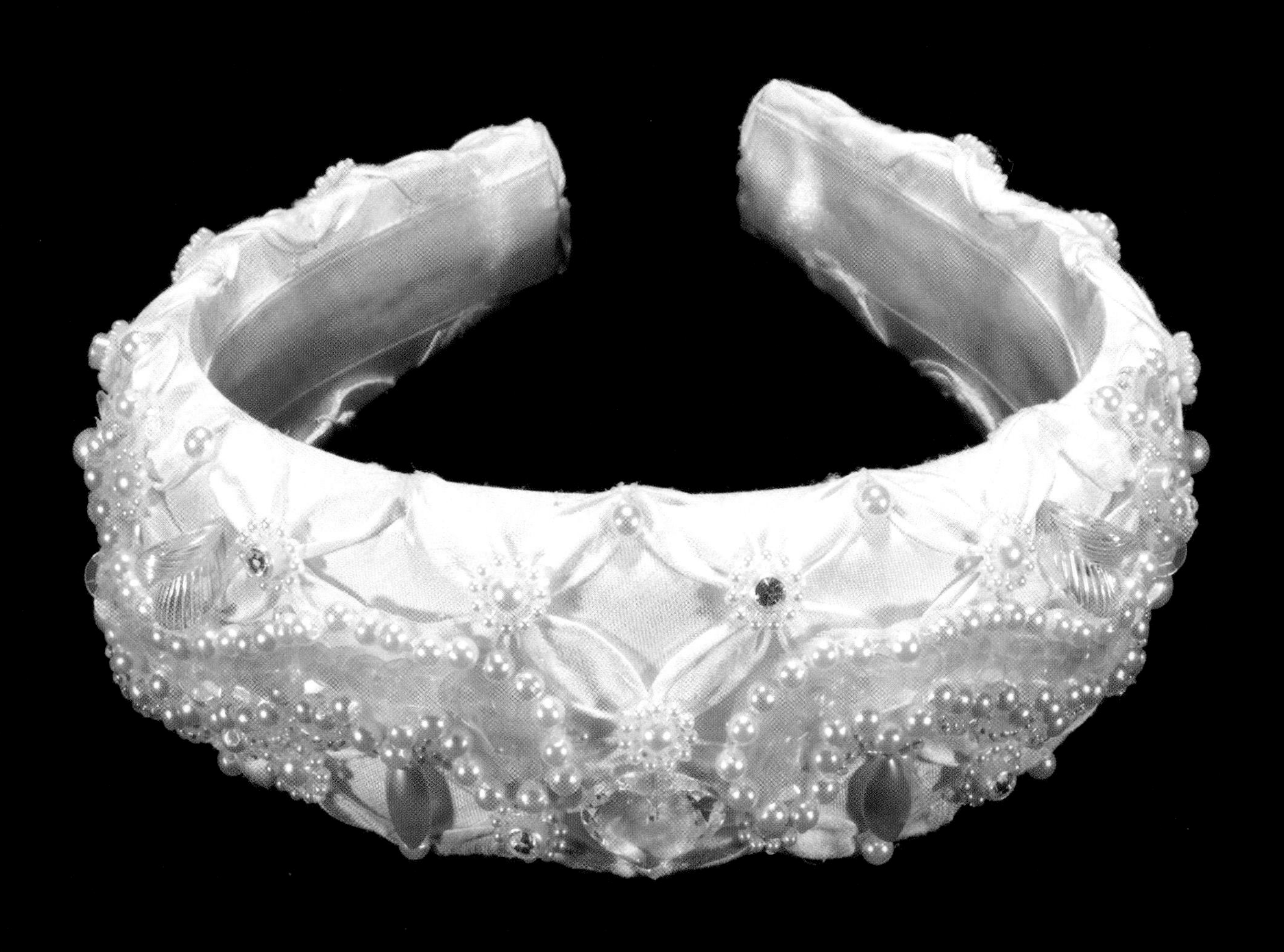

Plate 302

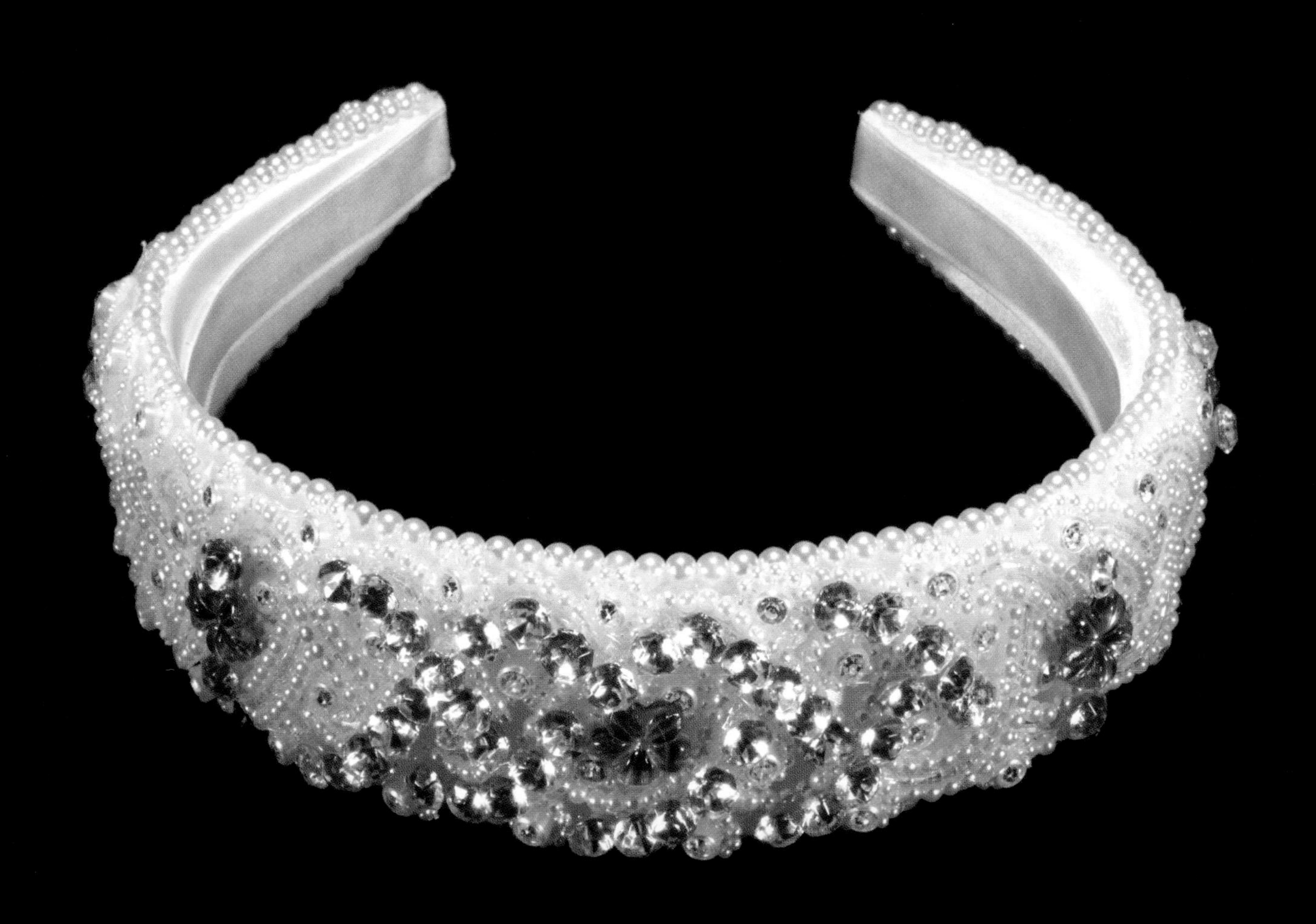

Plate 303

Plate 304

Plate 305

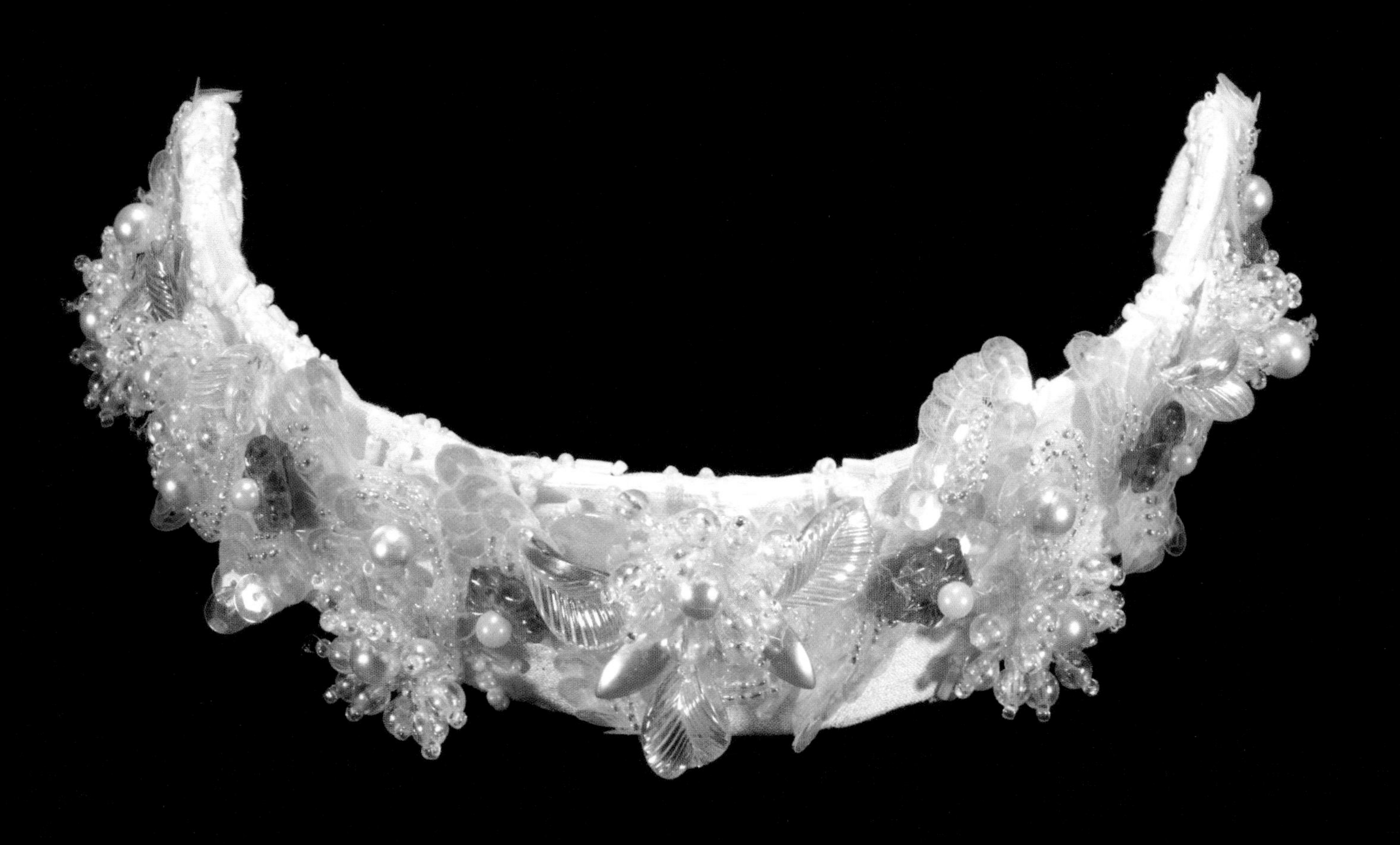

Plate 306

Headbands with Veil Attachment

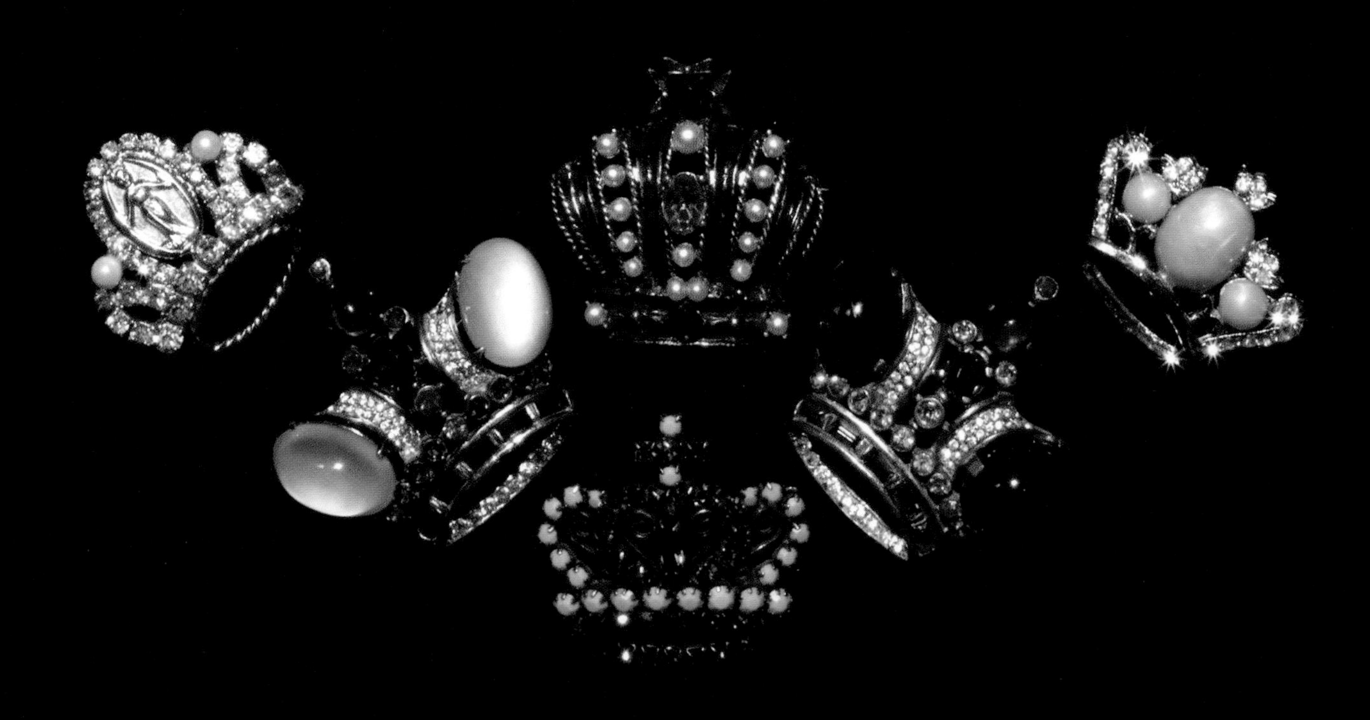

Plate 307

Plate 308

Plate 309

PLATE 310

Plate 311

Plate 312

Plate 313

PLATE 314

PLATE 315

Plate 316

PLATE 317

Plate 318

PLATE 319

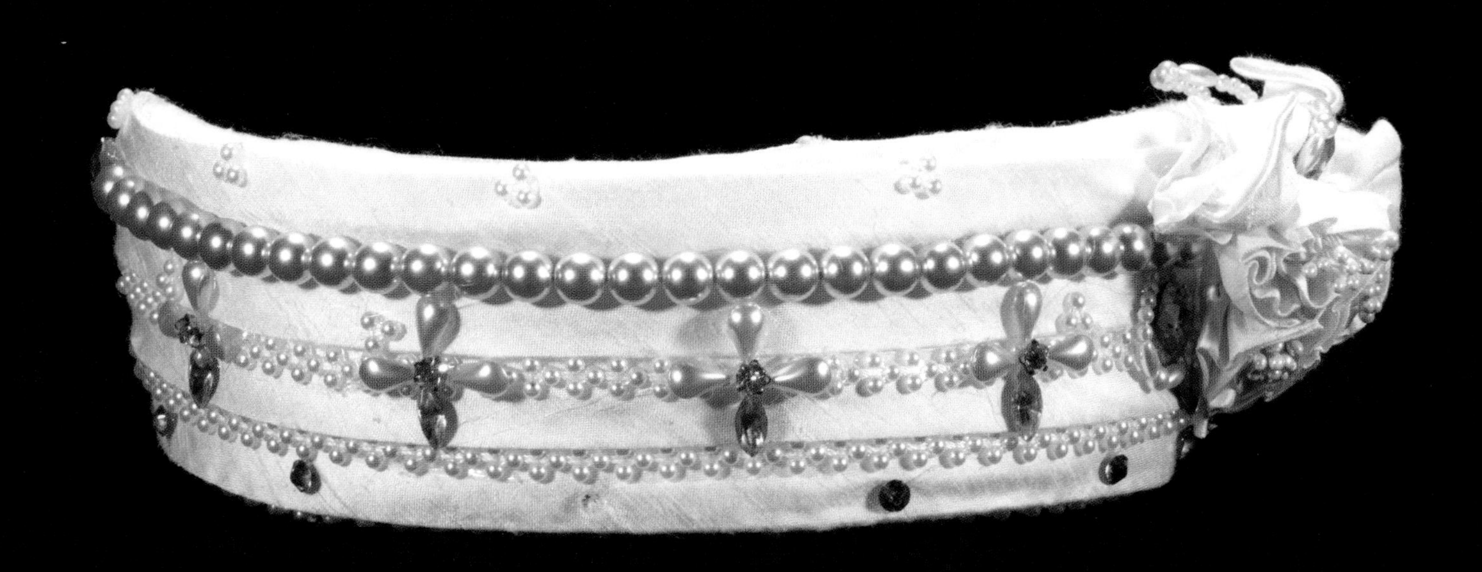

PLATE 320

Plate 321

Plate 322

PLATE 323

Plate 324

Plate 325

Plate 326

Plate 327

PLATE 328

Plate 329

Plate 330

Plate 331

PLATE 332

Plate 333

Plate 334

Full Circle Headbands

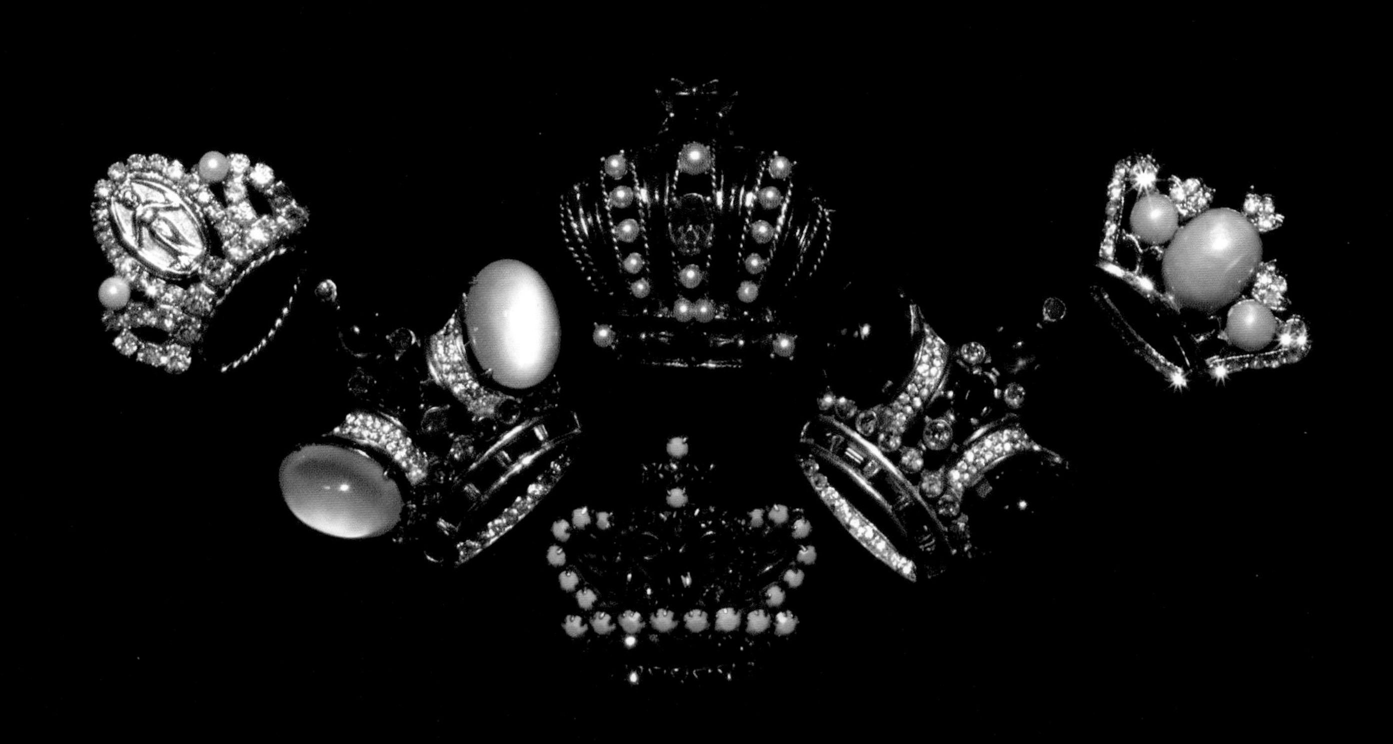

PLATE 335

Plate 336

PLATE 337

Plate 338

Plate 339

PLATE 340

PLATE 341

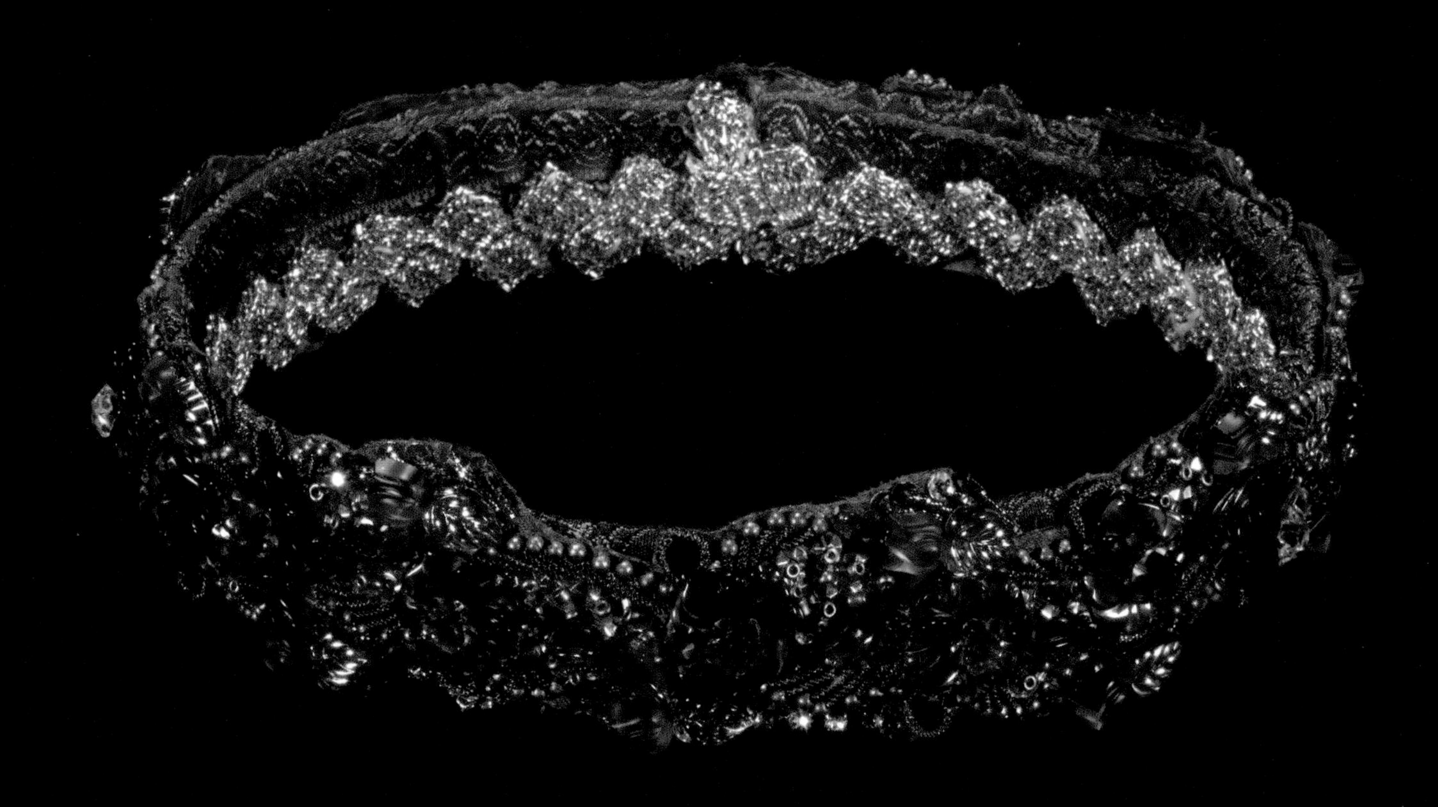

Plate 342

Plate 343

PLATE 344

PLATE 345

Plate 346

PLATE 347

Plate 348

PLATE 349

PLATE 350

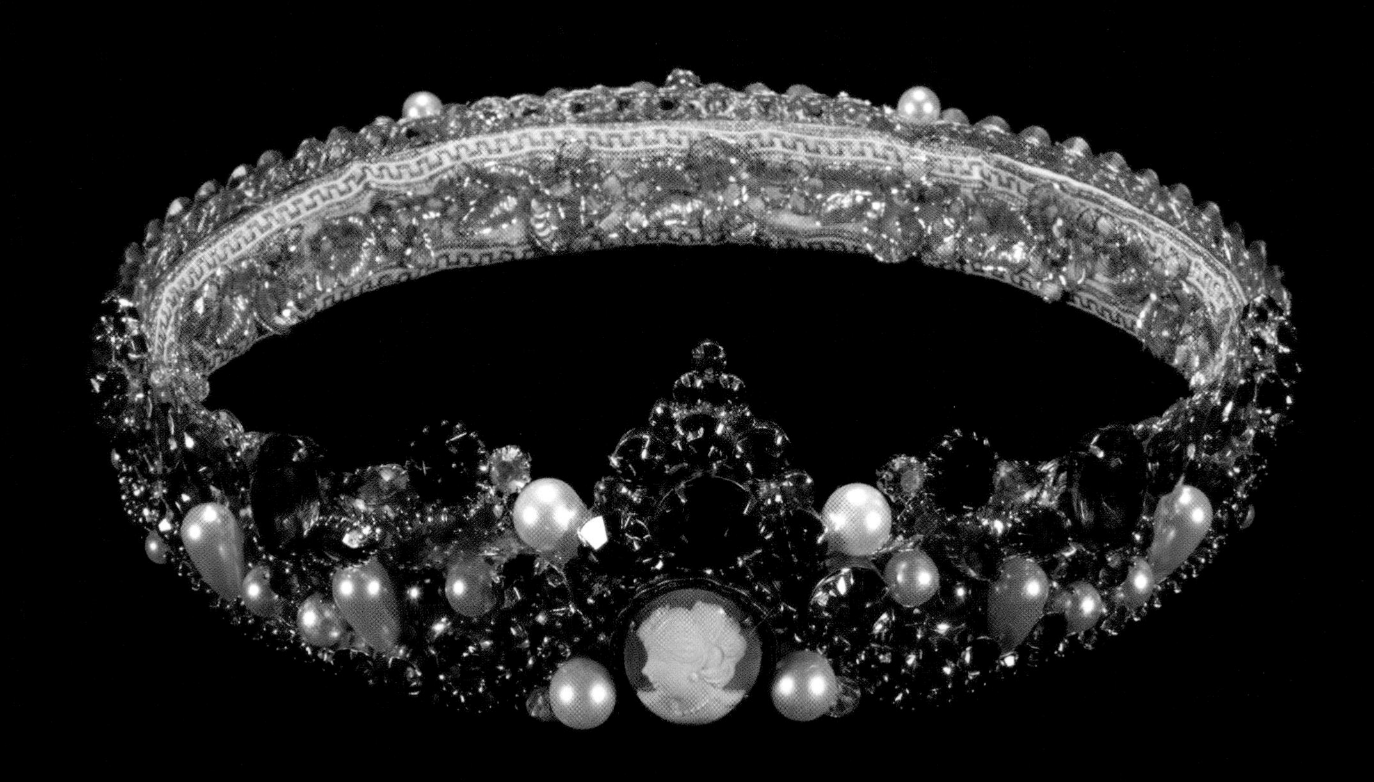

PLATE 351

Plate 352

PLATE 353

Plate 354

Plate 355

Plate 356

PLATE 357

Plate 358

Plate 359

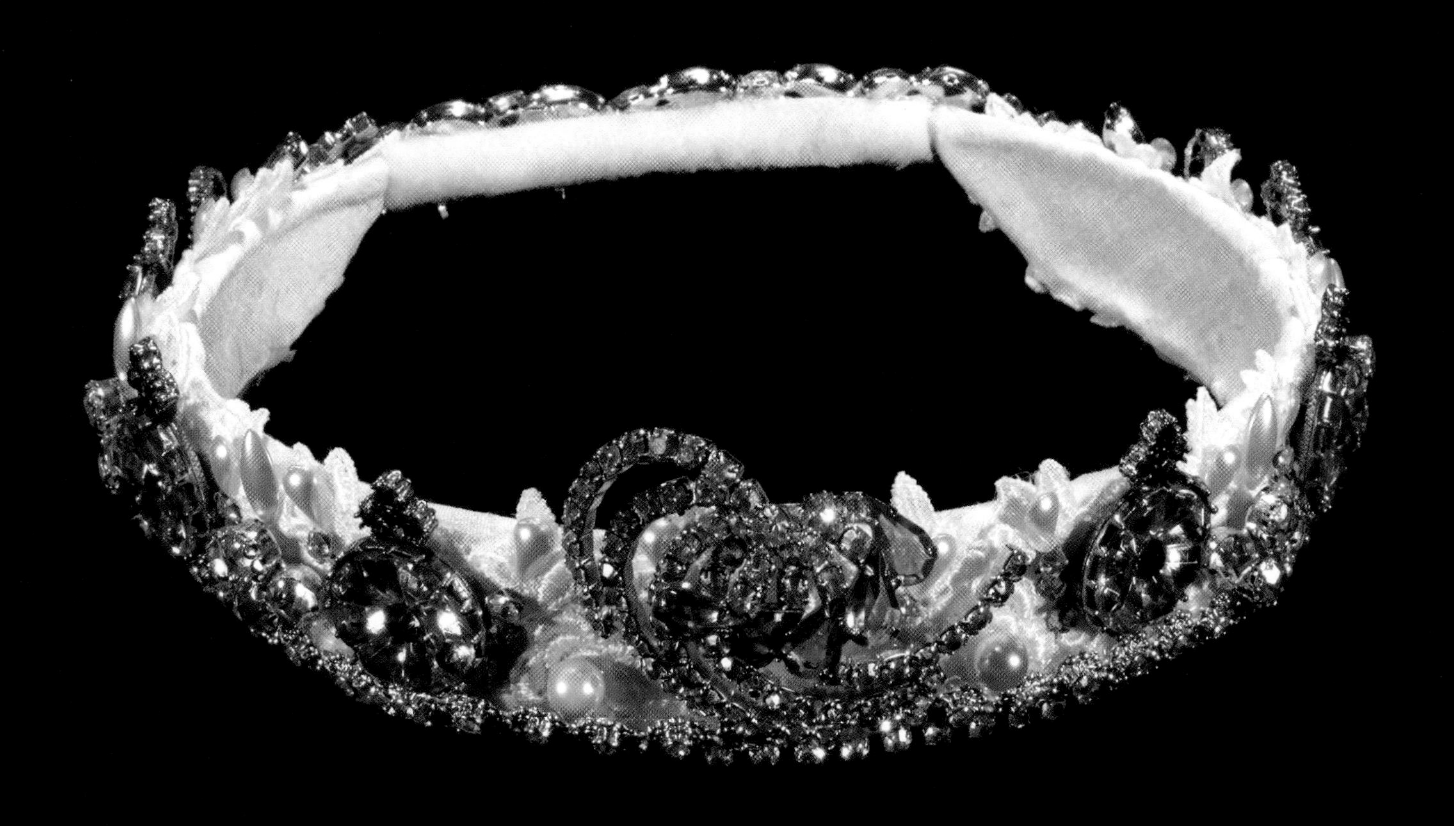

Plate 360

PLATE 361

PLATE 362

PLATE 363

PLATE 364

PLATE 365

Plate 366

Plate 367

Plate 368

Plate 369

Plate 370

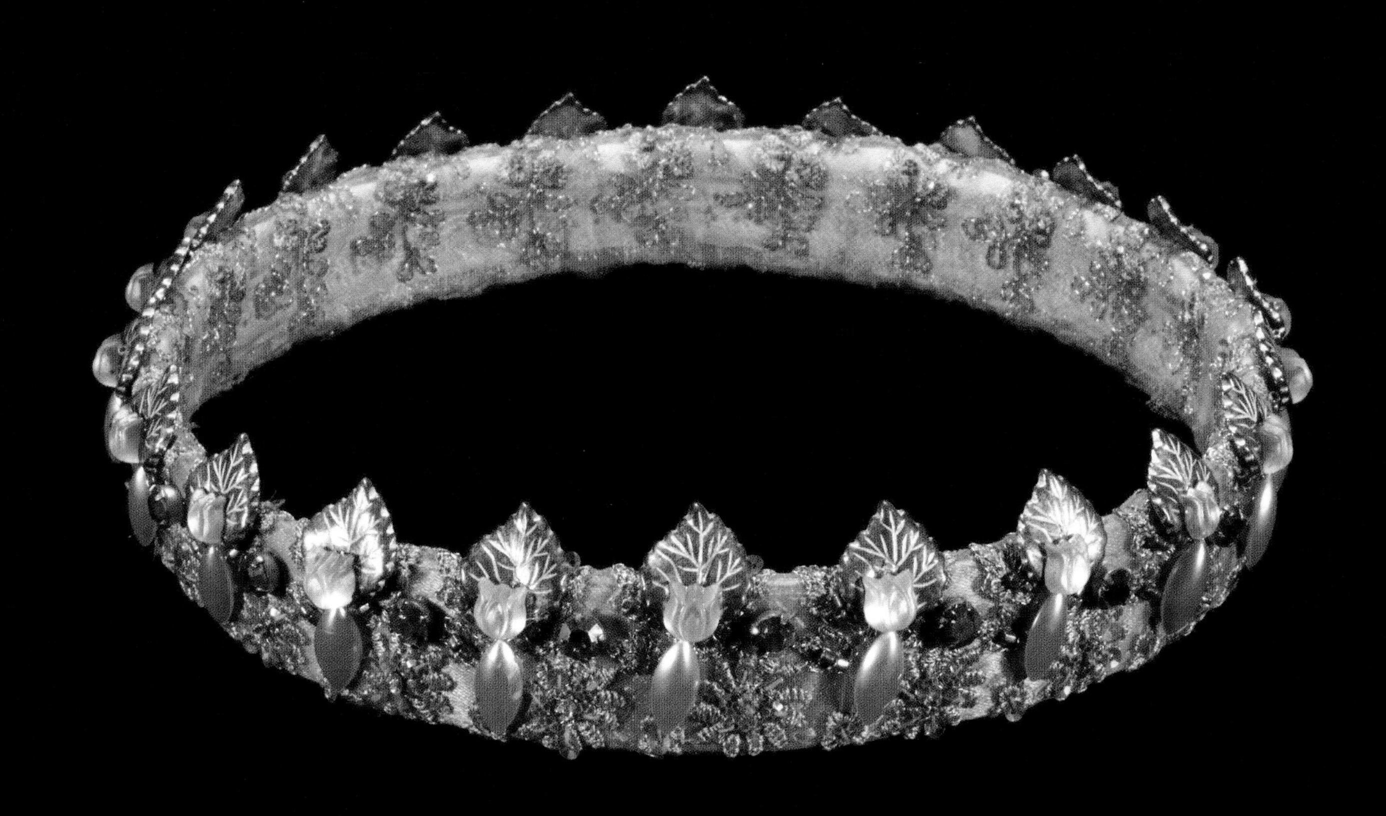

Plate 371

Plate 372

PLATE 373

Plate 374

Plate 375

PLATE 376

PLATE 377

PLATE 378

Plate 379

PLATE 380

Plate 381

PLATE 382

PLATE 383

Plate 384

PLATE 385

PLATE 386

PLATE 387

PLATE 388

Plate 389

Plate 390

Plate 391

PLATE 392

Plate 393

Plate 394

Plate 395

Plate 396

Plate 397

Plate 398

Hats

Plate 399

Plate 400

PLATE 401

Plate 402

PLATE 403

PLATE 404

Antique Tiaras

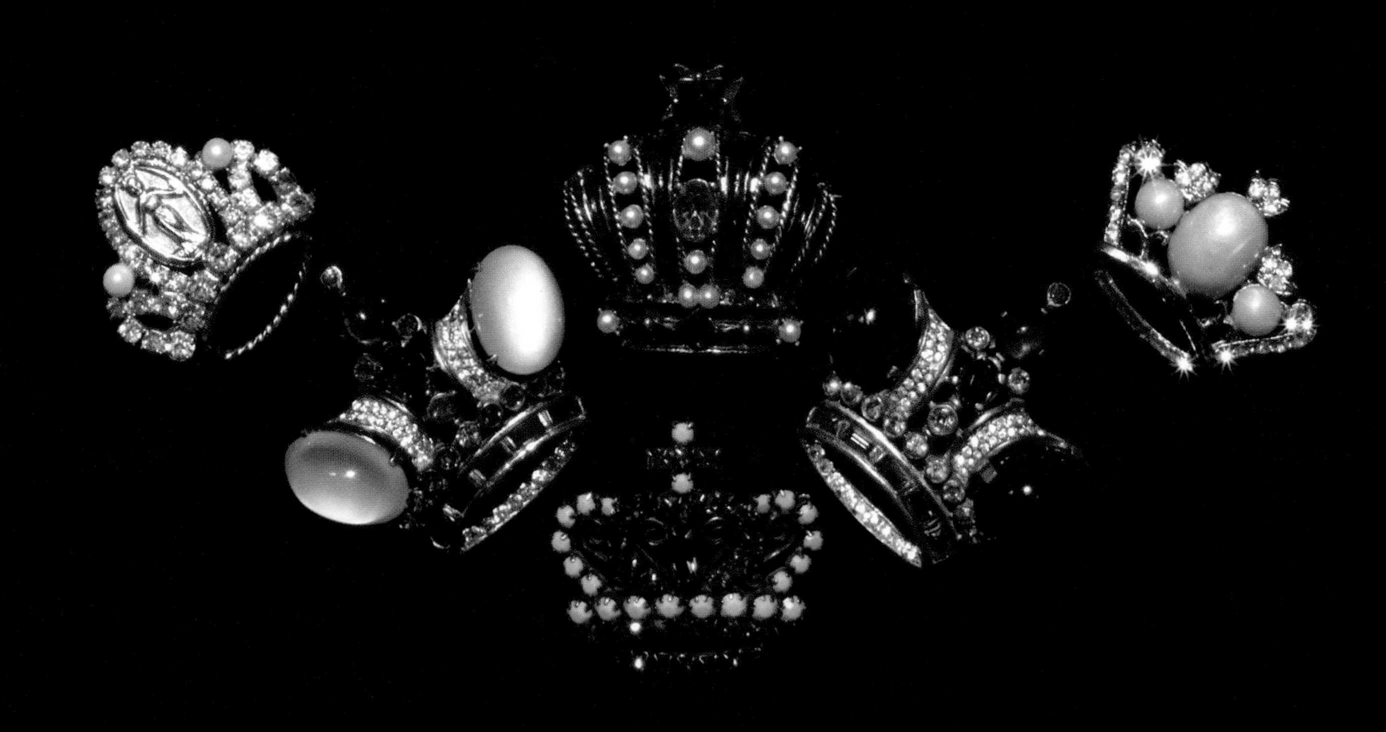

Plate 405

PLATE 406

PLATE 407

Plate 408

Plate 409

PLATE 410

Plate 411

PLATE 412

Beauty under glass

Prior to photography and scrapbooks, our ancestors recorded weddings with delicate displays. The bride's headpiece and other accessories were kept under a glass dome and proudly showcased in the parlor or boudoir. This tradition has been traced back to western France in the 19th century and endured throughout WWI.

We can surmise that the higher the class, the more elaborate the dome. The finest French clock and glassmakers made many such domes. Parents of the betrothed presented the couple with this precious keepsake.

Most dome displays have a wood base with a small cushion covered in velvet. On this, the bride's headpiece—made with wax flowers so it would be forever preserved—is mounted. Intertwining the headpiece may be other mementos: a brooch, a glove, a curl snipped from a true love's brow, a leaf or sheave of wheat. And as was the lore and romance of the Victorians, every token bore meaning. The sheave of wheat signified the gift of life. Rectangular mirrors reflected the years of engagement, whereas diamond-shaped mirrors promised fertility. Grapes were a blessing of prosperity and cherries warded off misfortune.

Not only the headpieces, but the assembly of these domes inspire me. I admire the sentiment and craftsmanship of an era where beauty was engrained in every ritual.

French Wedding Globes

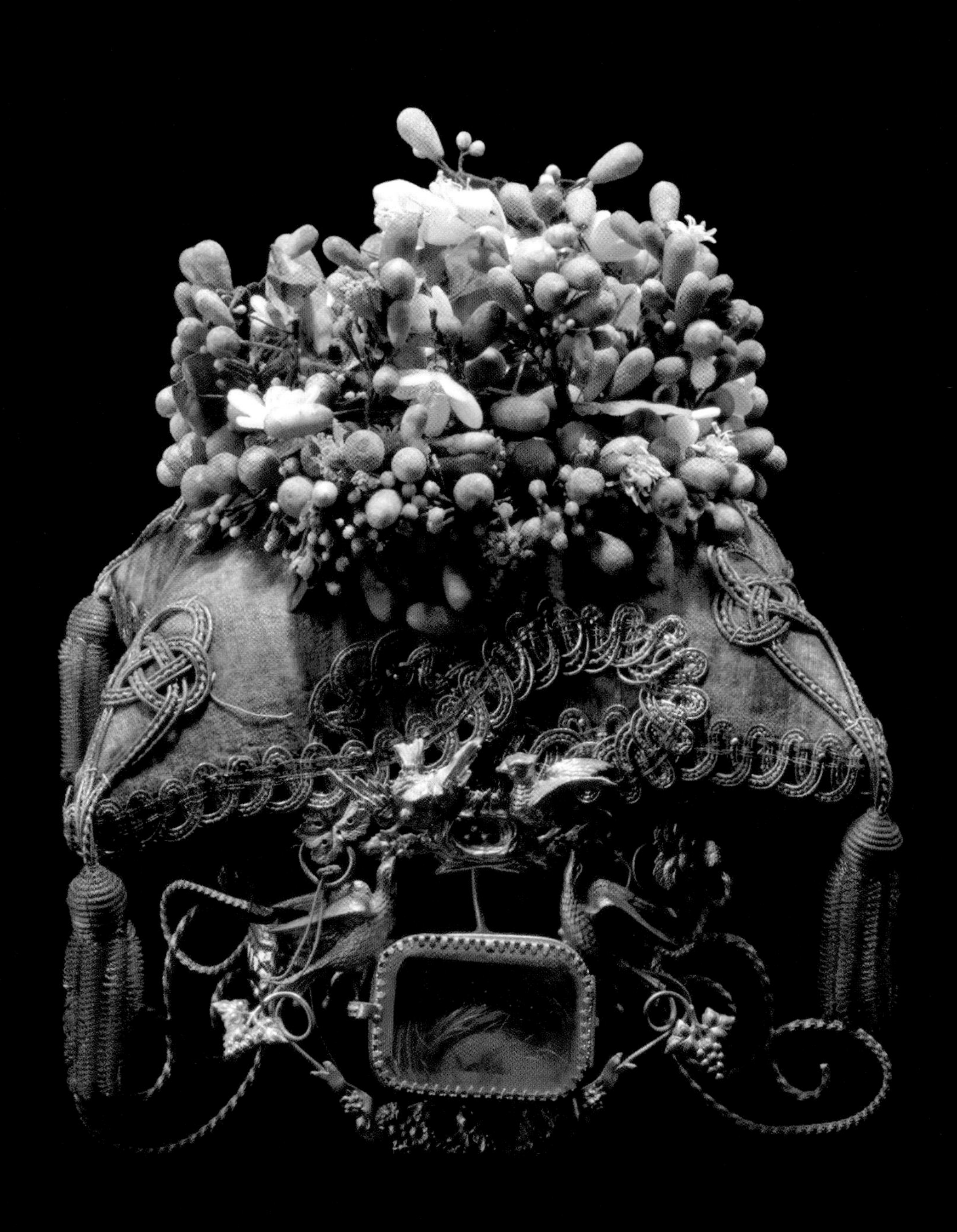

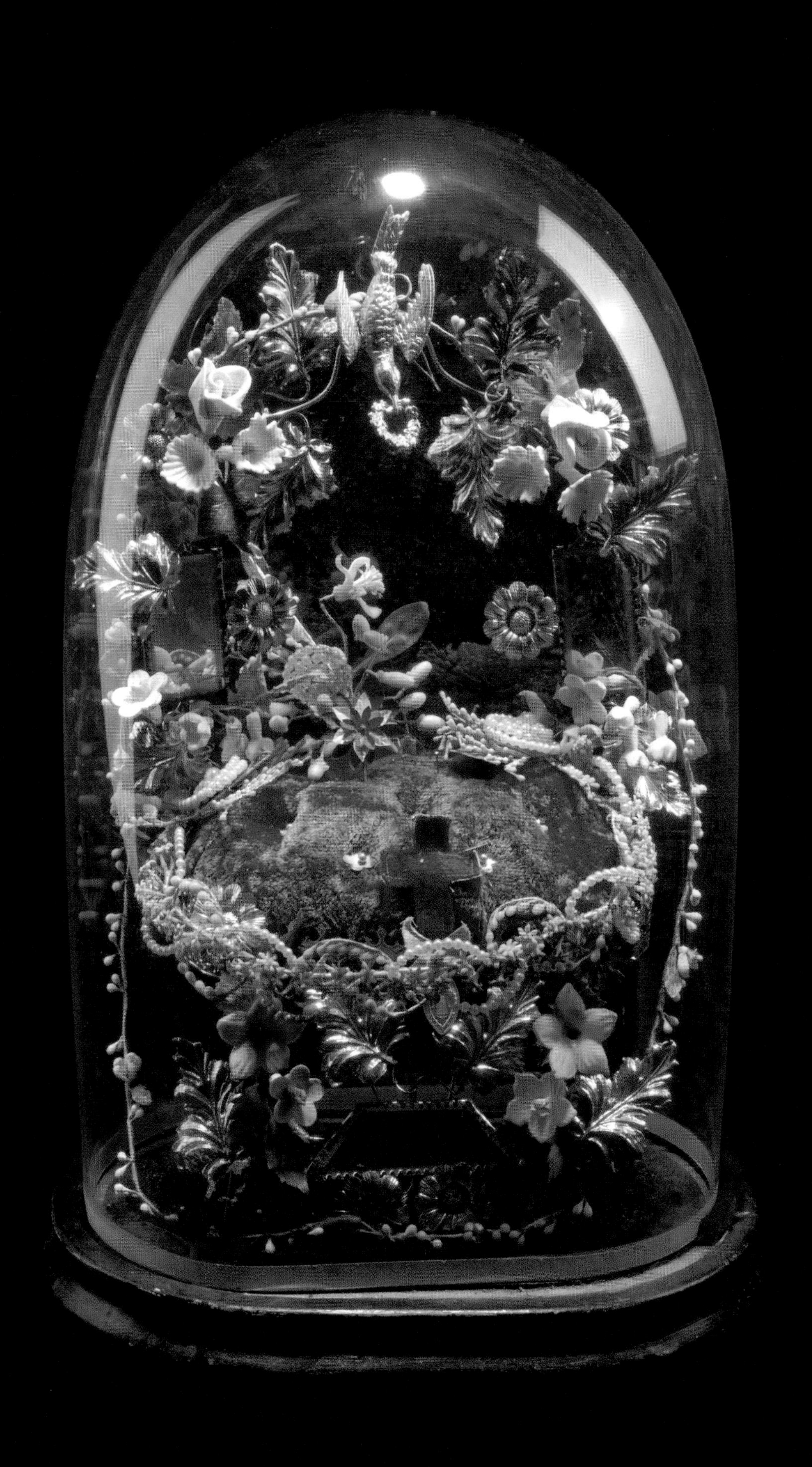

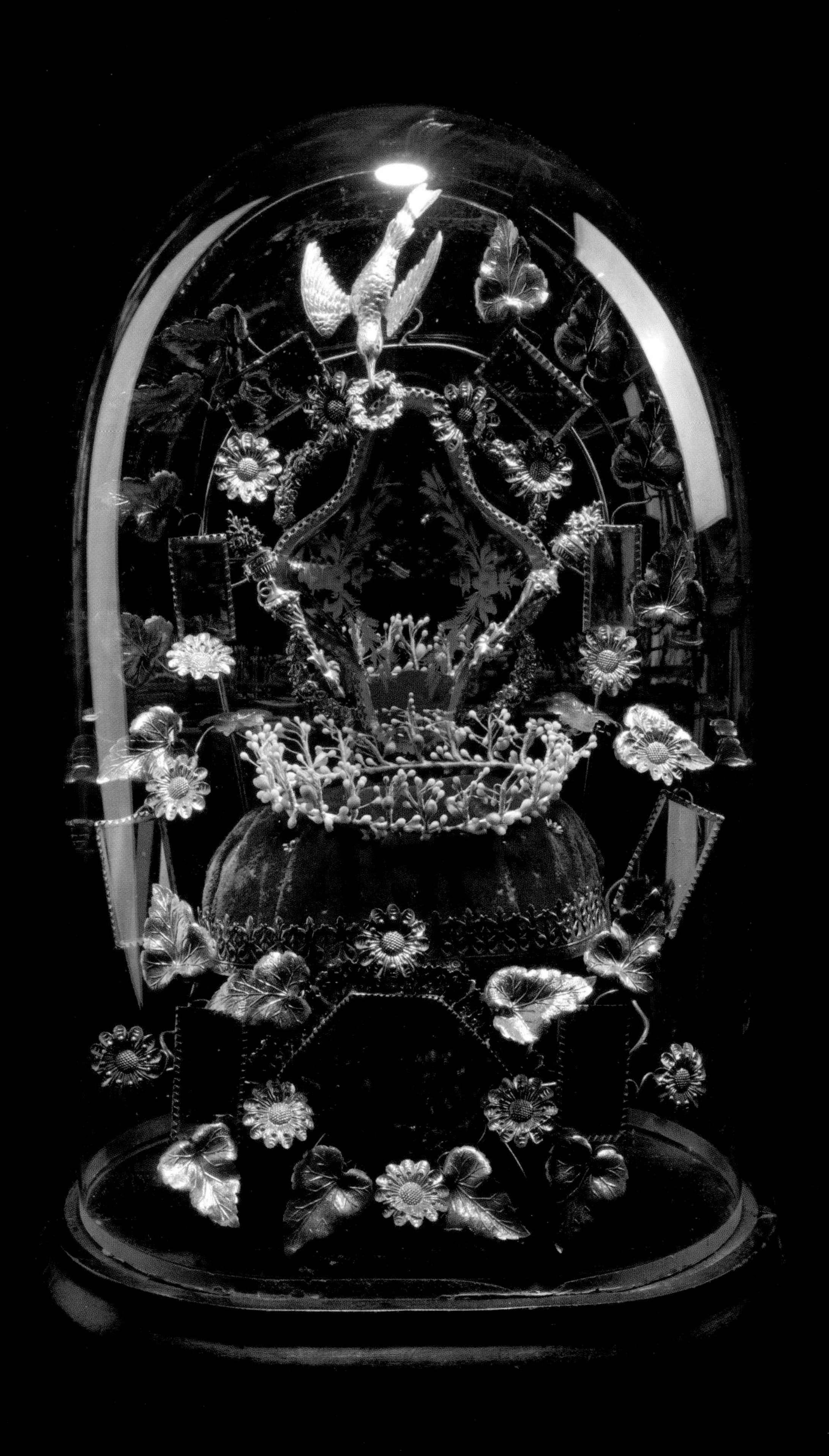

Resources

Glam by Pam, LLC
Seattle, WA
www.GlamByPam.net
info@glambypam.net
pc@glambypam.net

Exclusive headpieces, heirloom headpiece kits, book *Crowns*, vintage jewelry, flowers, gems, and other related fabulous materials.

For Your Inspirations

For Your Inspirations

For Your Inspirations

For Your Inspirations

For Your Inspirations

For Your Inspirations